the
entrepreneur's
GUIDE
to achieving financial freedom

"Having Jay on my team, gives me the freedom and confidence that allow me to dedicate my resources and time to running my business. Ever vigilant and straight-forward... his common sense approach is an asset to any small business."

— **Vincent Tolins**,
President Pro-Tech Plumbing & Heating

"Jay has been with us since 1998. Jay's guidance is always solid and he gives us confidence about our future. What impresses me the most about Jay is his uncanny ability to understand and anticipate our needs. After 18 years we have never seen Jay become complacent; he's constantly searching for new ideas."

— **Lawton Adam**s,
President Lawton Adams Construction

"I have always been impressed with the care Jay has taken to help me build success through life's challenges. His hard work and innovative ideas have proven invaluable."

—**Lori Fremaint**,
CEO Direct Mail of New York

"Jay has provided sound ideas and clarity for me and my family for over 15 years. He is innovative, insightful, and creative in any situation. I am extremely pleased."

— **Sigurd Feile**,
President Atlantic Nursery & Garden Shop

"I have known Jay now for more than 12 years. My satisfaction with him has developed from his organizational skills and his ability to explain complicated concepts. He treats your concerns as if it were his own. With Jay you can get the best of both worlds. He's a tireless professional who listens to your needs, but more importantly, he is a friend."

— **Joseph Minarik**, Vice President
Pro-Tech Plumbing & Heating

*These are the personal views of a select group of Jay Hochheiser's clients and may not represent the experience of other clients. These opinions are not indicative of future performance or results.

the
entrepreneur's
GUIDE
to achieving financial freedom

JAY E. HOCHHEISER, CFP®, CEPA

NEW YORK

NASHVILLE MELBOURNE

the entrepreneur's **GUIDE**
to achieving financial freedom

© 2017 JAY E. HOCHHEISER, CFP®, CEPA

Published in New York, New York, by Morgan James Publishing. Morgan James and The Entrepreneurial Publisher are trademarks of Morgan James, LLC.
www.MorganJamesPublishing.com

The Morgan James Speakers Group can bring authors to your live event. For more information or to book an event visit The Morgan James Speakers Group at www.TheMorganJamesSpeakersGroup.com.

Shelfie

A **free** eBook edition is available
with the purchase of this print book.

CLEARLY PRINT YOUR NAME ABOVE IN UPPER CASE

Instructions to claim your free eBook edition:
1. Download the Shelfie app for Android or iOS
2. Write your name in **UPPER CASE** above
3. Use the Shelfie app to submit a photo
4. Download your eBook to any device

ISBN 978-1-68350-146-6 paperback
ISBN 978-1-68350-154-1 eBook
ISBN 978-1-68350-153-4 hardcover
Library of Congress Control Number:
2016911248

Cover Design by:
Megan Whitney

Interior Design by:
Bonnie Bushman
The Whole Caboodle Graphic Design

In an effort to support local communities, raise awareness and funds, Morgan James Publishing donates a percentage of all book sales for the life of each book to Habitat for Humanity Peninsula and Greater Williamsburg.

Get involved today! Visit
www.MorganJamesBuilds.com

This book is dedicated to my wonderful wife Jill—without whose help and support my life is not possible. And to my two amazing children, Lee and Lauren; I can't imagine life without them. The amazing love we share inspires me and fuels my passion to ensure other families are truly protected and secure.

Table of Contents

Introduction

It's Harder Than Ever To Be A Successful Entrepreneur

To be a successful entrepreneur means you have built your career on working hard, making smart decisions, and, usually, learning from those decisions that weren't so smart. The motto of the entrepreneur is simple: "Adapt or die."

This motto has never been truer than it is today. The financial landscape of the business world has changed forever. The ripple effect of the Great Recession means that deals made today go for far less than they would have ten years ago. The pace of doing business is much more challenging, and financially, things are more unpredictable than ever. The new mantra, it seems, is, "Work harder for less."

The fact is, it has never been harder to be a successful entrepreneur. Customers are playing the float game to a greater degree than ever. People who used to pay you in thirty days are now paying you in ninety. On top of that, the Internet creates more competition, because it allows buyers to have more choices. In the past, buyers could only choose vendors within a limited geographical area. Now, depending on the product or service, buyers can order from anywhere in the world. The game has definitely changed.

In such an unforgiving market, there is no room for mistakes. However, financial success is no longer a matter of just adapting your business practices. It also means adapting financially—and the two don't always go hand in hand. More than ever, entrepreneurs need a higher level of security and financial protection in their own personal financial plans to weather the potential business cash flow storms that are likely to arise.

Maximizing your returns by making the best decisions with your resources comes down to one thing: disciplined, smart practices. And smart practices come from smart advice.

I've been working in financial services for thirty-two years. I began at age 22, when I started working for the Equitable Life Insurance Company. From there, I began to do comprehensive financial planning. I wanted to move into objective, fee-based planning, so I eventually left Equitable, and in 1996, I got my CFP – my certified financial planning designation. I started my own company that same year.

I approach financial planning a little differently than most financial planners. Most financial planners and advisors only look at your current life stage. All they're thinking about is accumulating money. They're not thinking about how much you're going to have to pay in taxes[1] later on, or how you're going to access that money.

Over my time in the financial services industry, I have seen so many smart and talented entrepreneurs make the same wrong financial decisions over and over again. Some of these wrong financial decisions are not major. Others, however, have the potential to derail one's lifestyle in retirement completely. The wrong financial decision could translate to hundreds of thousands or even millions of dollars lost over your lifetime.

There is absolutely no reason to continue making these financial mistakes—because I know how to avoid them. As a seasoned financial advisor, and a very creative financial strategist, I've discovered what makes for the best financial future—and those are the strategies I am going to share with you.

In this book, you will learn many efficient methods for making the most of your money. You will learn about strategies to help you pay fewer taxes over your lifetime, along with creative opportunities to bring you more money, *and* let you use and enjoy that money more fully. You will discover how to align your financial vision with your business partner and avoid common financial mistakes.

The insight you'll gain from this book could unlock resources you aren't even aware you have. It can mean the difference between financial stability and financial freedom; the difference between working just to live and enjoying your life to its fullest potential.

---

1   Guardian, its subsidiaries, agents, and employees do not provide tax, legal, or accounting advice. Consult your tax, legal, or accounting professional regarding your individual situation.

This book will provide you with the education and understanding to help change your way of thinking about the best steps to achieve financial freedom. You will learn how to enhance the value of your resources so you can enjoy a better life for you and your family, not only in retirement, but in all stages of your life. This book will show you strategies you can implement when you are forty or fifty that can put yourself in a better financial position by the time you are sixty or seventy.

As a successful entrepreneur, you've worked hard and adapted wisely in your business. Now, do the same with your finances and your planning. In doing so, you will have a greater sense of security, and less stress along the way.

Be sure to check out "**The Financial Freedom Scorecard**" toward the end of the book!

Regards,
Jay E. Hochheiser, CFP ®, CEPA

Chapter 1

Why Your iPhone Won't Give You Financial Freedom

We all thought technology would make life easier, and in many ways it has. Today it is easier than ever to communicate, to share ideas, and to stay connected. You can order dinner, call your cousin in Russia, and book a weekend getaway to Tahiti all in one fell swoop.

But this technology business isn't all roses. As much as smart devices have streamlined tasks in everyday life, they have also muddied the waters of information. Between the Internet, newspapers and magazines, radio, and TV, we have a million voices yapping at us every day with tips on the best way to live, the best way to make decisions.

Amidst all of that noise, how can anyone figure out what is truly the "best way" to do anything?

With a million voices at your beck and call, how do you know which ones will actually help you?

Knowing which strategies and financial products are best for your particular situation is a daunting task. That old adage, "He who has access to information wins," no longer applies. Rather, the new adage is: "He who filters best through noise, avoids mistakes, and capitalizes on opportunities wins."

To answer this problem, most people tune into "general advice," or the advice that is available through mainstream news and programs. Whatever they say on the morning news is what will work best for you, right?

Well, not always. Mainstream TV and radio shows are called "mainstream" for a reason. They are designed to give out cookie-cutter advice and information, and content is generally maximized for entertainment value. Normally, any "tips and tricks" are given in broad terms without any consideration for what the entrepreneur's own personal situation may be.

Even if the "mainstream" information is, indeed, good information, one big question remains: "Is it good information for *you*?"

The source might be accurate, but you may be the wrong audience.

Consider this: Today, if you earn more than $116,623 in this country, you are in the top 10 percent of all US household incomes. If you earn more than $161,579, you are in the top 5 percent of US household incomes, and if you earn more than $343,926, you are in the top 1 percent of US household incomes.

Moreover, today, 90 percent of the wealth in this country is owned by 10percent of the people.[2]

If you were in the media business and producing TV shows focused on investment or financial advice, which audience would you want to appeal to? 1 percent of the population, or 99 percent of the population? Of course, you would want the biggest population as a target audience for your business, and you would adjust your message for that demographic.

And therein lies the flaw of heeding the advice pushed out by the mass media: If you are in the top 1 percent, 5 percent, or even 10 percent—if you are a high income earner—then you, my friend, are the wrong audience.

Most of the information and advice preached in the media is aimed at that 99 percent of US households, and therefore may not be relevant to the entrepreneur making $500,000, $1 million, or $2 million per year. It may help the person making $50,000 or maybe even $100,000 per year, who is living in a low-taxed, low cost-of-living state and who is probably not going to build up millions of dollars of wealth over his or her lifetime. But how does that help you?

Now, you may be someone who is not swayed by what they see or hear in the news. Even so, if you have a partner, then you aren't making financial decisions on your own. You can turn off the TV, but you can't tune out your partner or family members, all of whom have a huge influence on what you do with your money. So you have to ask: where does your spouse get their information? How can you be sure that the two of you are on the same page financially?

---

2   IRS data in December 2012 Kiplinger's worksheet

All of these factors add to the complexity of the simple question, "What should I do?"

Moreover, misinformation is not the only obstacle on the entrepreneur's journey to financial freedom. Another huge factor is something that is infrequently discussed, let alone understood: tax laws. Government's frequently change tax laws! Tax laws are constantly evolving, which means that what was good for you at one time may not work so well now. The rules keep changing and your job—or the job of your advisors—is to make all the necessary adjustments.

Adding to this complicated situation is the wide array of products offered by financial advisors. I constantly see entrepreneurs trying various products and strategies, quickly accumulating what I call "the junk drawer" of financial decisions. Everybody has a junk drawer. It's that place where you put all

of the odds and ends that you think you'll need some day, but are not quite sure what to use them for in the present. So you stash them away, and before you know it, you have a collection of disparate pieces that you really have no idea where they belong or how they are beneficial.

This is exactly what can happen with financial decisions. Entrepreneurs buy different financial products from different advisors at different times. They may invest in products based on hype, their neighbor's opinion, or something that they read. Over time, all of these decisions and investments amount to a whole lot of confusion. Each separate financial decision is made at a different time with no view or plan for the greater good. You have no idea how many of these items can or will be used to protect and grow your wealth and enhance your life later on.

Moreover, all these decisions may not just be confusion and junk—some of these products and strategies might actually be harmful. Entrepreneurs might not be able to fully recover from that harm, or their financial freedom may not be what it could have been had they been equipped with custom-tailored solutions for their particular situation.

As time goes on, and as more of these odds and ends come into your possession, the less coordination there is between all of these products. They are all supposed to serve one purpose: creating your financial freedom. Instead, you're left with the junk drawer.

If you're like most people, you put off sorting through that junk drawer. Who has the time for that anyway? But I'm here to tell you that there is a way to cut through the noise. There is a way to clean out the junk drawer—and no, it's not an app on your iPhone! More powerful than any technology or product is the person—or people—you have on your side.

The trick to achieving financial success is to find an advisor who can guide you on your financial journey, an advisor who can bring their expertise in finance to enhance the efforts of your own business savvy. I'm not talking about a multitude of advisors each working independently in their own cocoon. I'm talking about a team with a coordinated view of your big picture.

When's the last time all of your advisors were in the room with you, talking about you and your financial journey?

Usually, the answer is, "Never."

If this is your answer too, then it's time to consider a new approach.

In order for an entrepreneur to be truly successful, you need to have a great advisory team. As a business owner, there needs to be coordination not only with products and strategies you may be employing, but also coordination among your advisors.

Finding an advisor you can trust in this uncertain world is a challenge, to say the least. After all, you want someone who looks holistically at your big picture, who is not just pushing an agenda of selling their particular product or service. It may be challenging for you to find an advisor with whom you can build a long-term trusting relationship, and who has the big picture covered.

To find that person, you must ask yourself: **Who's looking out for me twenty years down the road? Who will look ahead to see how all of this will work out and what it all means?**

Most advisors only focus on today or tomorrow. They are not looking down the road to see how the entrepreneur is going to access the wealth that they're building in an efficient manner. Many advisors say, "Don't worry about later until later." But later comes quicker than you think, and you may lose creative options by not being future-focused.

Finding your "big picture" advisor is the first step toward financial freedom. This book will take you the rest of the way, by looking at big, future-focused questions:

- How are you going to best utilize the resources that you have built?
- Are you going to get hammered in taxes later, and should you be planning for that now?
- What is your vision in five years', ten years', and twenty years' time?

- Are you and your partner on the same page, financially?
- How do you filter the noise?
- If you have any of these questions or concerns, read on. The following pages contain the information you need to make a big impact on your life, and on the lives of those you love.

Chapter 2

Cash Flow is King

You have probably heard that cash is king, but that's only half the story. It's not cash that is king, but *cash flow*. And when we talk about cash flow, I only mean *positive* cash flow! Negative cash flows stinks!

Positive cash flow rules the kingdom. On the opposite end of the spectrum is, of course, negative cash flow, which is more like the court jester. While a sense of humor is always a positive quality, who wants to be a laughing stock? No one. Thus, we all want to maintain positive cash flow.

The first basic elements of cash flow are the same two elements that create a sound financial plan: budgeting and saving.

Let's tackle saving first. How much are you saving? In this day and age, teachers like to say that there is no wrong answer. Unfortunately, in this case, there are many wrong answers, and only one right answer. The golden target for savings is 15-20 percent of your gross income—income meaning the amount after your business expenses are deducted from revenue, but before personal income taxes are taken out. 15-20 percent of that income needs to be saved away every salary check, every draw check, every time.

Deciding where you register in the 15-20 percent range comes down to your history. For someone who is new to their business, saving 15 percent right out of the gate is very good. If someone is more established in their career and has not built the kind of wealth they should have along the way, they may need to go up to 20-25 percent. If you are at a point in your business where your projected income is uncertain, you really want to be hitting that 20-25 percent number—or even a little higher, if possible. I know this can be challenging, but it is critical to achieving financial freedom.

Typically, an entrepreneur's best rate of return may be investing cash flow back into his/her business. I strongly recommend that entrepreneurs take this approach—but not at the cost of building personal wealth. While you're trying to grow a business, you're also trying to enjoy a lifestyle and build personal wealth through the income from your profitable business. If you're not taking money out of the business, investing, or saving for yourself personally, you're defeating the purpose. I see business owners pumping more and more money into their business and never taking any out for their own personal net worth. That is a mistake.

If you as a business owner are making $1 million a year between salary and profits, then you should be saving $150,000 a year for yourself. If you're just saving $50,000 a year and using the rest to reinvest, reinvest, reinvest, well... hopefully the years of reinvesting start to pay off at some point. But you have to be aware that you're only saving five percent of your gross income – and that means you're setting yourself up for potential hardship in the future.

You might be thinking you can sell the business for a high multiple and all your prayers will be answered – and that could happen. However, it's also very possible that it will never happen. Most businesses do not get sold that way. Therefore, you must save that 15 percent-20 percent of your gross income. This includes whatever you put into your 401(k), pensions, investment accounts, whole life policies, or whatever else you're doing. It all counts.

Paying yourself first is one of the most basic financial fundamentals, but many people seem to overlook it. That's why automating all of your savings can be a magic bullet!

The more you make, the more you spend. If you pay yourself first, you'll be assured of putting money away for you and your family before you pay all your other bills. Even better, you can automate your savings. Have the bank transfer 15-20 percent to your savings as soon as it hits your account. Automating your savings is one of the major keys to financial freedom, and with today's technology it is easier than ever. By automating your savings, you save more money.

It takes balance to invest both in yourself and in your business. It's not an easy balance, but it is a balance that can be achieved.

That's where budgeting comes in. Creating a smart budget is the way to meet that 15-20 percent goal.

"Budgeting" does not mean, "cutting out anything that could be construed as fun, luxurious, or enjoyable." On the contrary, if you deem something fun, luxurious, or enjoyable to be of value, then you should use your resources on it. But I bet that unless you make a practice of budgeting, your money isn't just being used for what you value. Instead, your money is going to superfluous expenditures.

When I have clients go through an exercise of completing a cash flow worksheet, they are often shocked to find they are spending so much on "x." The upside is that they have no problems reducing that amount, because they feel "x" is not worth the money they are spending on it. In this way, budgeting can actually be a very therapeutic practice.

Rather than finding ways to skimp, you are cutting out the excess fat and taking more control over your resources.

In other words, you are making smart decisions.

If you really want to save more, it is vital to know where you are spending your money. Once you know this, you can prioritize your cash-flow decisions. This takes coordination with whoever else is a part of the budget. Full disclosure: While many entrepreneurs find working on a budget with their spouse to be enlightening and very helpful, others have found it painful and dread it.

I'm with the former party. In my family, we go through the cost of our lifestyle and modify the budget as warranted. We keep it enjoyable by making it into a fun event with wine, cheese, and a festive mood. Then, we go about the business of accounting for the credit card bills, the wants, the needs, and all other purchases we've made. By doing this, we are able to consciously and collaboratively make decisions on the bigger expenditures and take the stress out of the process.

The greatest wonder of this budgeting party is that when you do it, money stops disappearing like it does when you don't pay close attention. Moreover, once you're on track, you will have a tremendous feeling of accomplishment knowing that you are in control of your own financial destiny.

It doesn't matter how much you make. A budget and savings will always take you to the next level. So get on board with budgeting and establish your reign as the positive cash flow king.

Chapter 3

Protecting the Precious

We all have one thing in our lives that we treasure above all else. For most, it's not a Ferrari, it's not a vacation home on Cape Cod, it's not even a business. At the end of the day, all of it—the material goods, the trips, even the job—is there to support one thing, and one thing only: your family. They are, to use *Lord of the Rings* lingo, your "precious," and like the all-powerful "one ring to rule them all" in that fantasy tale, you would protect and defend your family until your very last breath.

As an entrepreneur, your most powerful weapon for protecting your family is your ability to go out and earn a living.

But while you are earning that living, **who is protecting you?**

Most life goals that entrepreneurs would like to accomplish, for themselves and for their families, are based on their ability to generate an income. If the ability to generate an income ceases, then most of their goals and dreams disappear with it. It's a heavy burden to bear. However, there are ways of transferring this weight to another entity. The burden of protecting your family doesn't have to rest on your shoulders—and in fact, it shouldn't.

If you want to "protect the precious"—if you want to be fully protected from losses and life's uncertainties—then you have to safeguard your income and assets. And that comes down to having the proper insurance and documents in place.

Think of "insurance" as shorthand for "replacement value." Insurance works by replacing what it protects. For an entrepreneur, unexpected disasters, accidents, or illness can spell financial ruin for the business—and even more so for the family. But the right insurance can eliminate many of those threats.

The right insurance, structured correctly, can protect you from unexpected events so that your family and your lifestyle, hopes, and dreams will never be affected.

Insurance is not a new concept. I mentioned a Ferrari earlier because many of us can relate to the excitement of owning a special car—and to the necessity of buying car insurance. Let's say you've worked hard for the ability to afford that Ferrari. Once you purchase it, you want to get the best insurance coverage to protect your investment. Should anything happen to that Ferrari, you know that you will be able to continue riding in style because insurance will repair the damage, or replace the car if it is stolen.

The irony is that while people will spend good money to protect their Ferrari, they will not give the same consideration to themselves or their family. They will buy insurance to fully protect a $350,000 car, but they can't fathom doing the same for their livelihood, which may be in the multi-millions.

Why is that?

Quite simply, it's because insurance isn't sexy. Wills and trusts? What a buzzkill. It's not pleasant to think about the possibility of being out of work, nor is it fun to pay those monthly premiums. However, life can be unpredictable. It would be foolish, if not downright dangerous, to ignore the question, *What will I do if I can't work?*

Benjamin Franklin once said, "It is a strange anomaly that men should be careful to insure their houses… and yet neglect to insure their lives, surely the most important of all to their families, and far more subject to loss."

Mr. Franklin has a point, doesn't he? It seems uncanny that when protecting their income and their family, many people settle for far less than full replacement value, and less even than what they really need in order to have security.

My son gave my wife and I quite a scare when he was born ten weeks early, weighing only two and a half pounds. He hadn't fully developed yet, and he had to wear a sleep apnea monitor because he didn't always breathe while sleeping. During the two months we waited while our son grew stronger in the hospital, my wife and I were constantly on edge. In this trying time, I took off work in order to focus on my family. Finally, the doctor gave us the all-clear and we brought our new infant son home.

I was elated to have my family safe and together. However, those two months off of work amounted to a mountain of phone calls, correspondence, and paperwork to catch up on. As if my wife didn't have enough on her shoulders, she asked how she could help me transition back to work, and kindly took on the task of paying all of the bills.

I'll never forget the night she came into my office with a look of total shock on her face. She handed two invoices over to me—our bills for disability insurance.

"That's unbelievable," she said, referring to the amount in bold at the end of the statement. "Do we really have to pay all of this?"

"No, of course not," I replied. "But if I'm disabled, what are you willing to give up?"

She was silent for a moment, considering all of her options. Finally, she replied, "You know what? I think I'll pay them."

Now ask yourself: If something happened that put you or your partner out of work, what are you willing to give up?

It's easy to cast off something that isn't necessarily of use to you in the moment. But it is far better to invest now in order to be protected in the future, rather than exposing yourself to the devastation of loss.

That's why disability insurance is the first line of defense when it comes to protection.

Disability insurance is no fun to pay for, but it is critical. If your greatest asset is your ability to go out and earn a living, and you can't do that, your whole world changes. However, this is something most entrepreneurs don't want to think about.

If you go off on a two-week vacation, I guarantee that you're still making calls and dealing with things. What if, because of an unexpected illness or injury, you went away for a month? What if you went away for six months? Would you still have a business to come back to and what would your income turn in to? That's what disability insurance does – it insures your income stream if there is a time when you are unable to go to work.

I once explained it to a client this way: Let's say you get offered two jobs. At one job, you'll get $750,000 per year, but if you become disabled, you would receive $0. In the other job, they would pay you $743,000 per year, but if you become disabled, you would receive $250,000 per year tax-free. Which compensation plan would you select?

The answer is obvious, right? You would take the one with disability insurance. In the grand scheme of things, it really isn't a huge expense. In this example, it would cost you less than 1 percent of your income to protect 33 percent of your livelihood after tax—the equivalent of approximately 50 percent of your net after tax income..

A good advisor can help you find the best protection for the best cost. However, it isn't always about finding the *smallest* check to write. It's about securing the *best protection*. Moreover, it's not just your own life that you have to consider. What if you have a child in college, and his or her dreams are dependent on you being able to help pay for that degree? If you're disabled, your child might go from a top school to community college. Now are you sure that disability premium is too expensive to pay for?

My son is all grown up now and in his first year at University of Michigan. It's a great school, but it's not cheap. He had dreams of going to a prestigious school, and I'm proud that I can support his hard work. But what if I had become disabled a few years ago and didn't have coverage to help support me? I might have had to say, "Son, I love you, but I can't work anymore. I can't afford to send you to the college you worked so hard to get accepted to." Perhaps I wouldn't even have had the funds to send him to any college at all.

God willing, you should never be faced with such a circumstance—but you cannot control what happens. **The only thing you can control is how your family might be affected—or protected. If it's in your power to protect you and your family, why wouldn't you do so?**

Should anything happen to you that would prevent you from working, disability insurance provides income to help support you in the interim. In addition, there are policies designed specifically to protect your business should you be prevented from working. These shorter-term policies, called overhead expense policies, cover necessities such as hiring a replacement if you need to take a leave of absence. They're designed to provide an infusion of income to the business to help cover some of the overhead. That's not personal disability insurance; it's business disability insurance.

Just like in life, many unexpected issues can arise in business. Disability insurance is one resource to protect against a temporary inability to work. But what if something happened that meant the breadwinner would never go back to work? What if tragedy struck and your family was completely on their own? How would they get by?

The answer to this question is simple: life insurance.

Life insurance functions in three ways. First, life insurance ensures that your beneficiaries are able to maintain their current lifestyle in the event of the premature death of a breadwinner. Life insurance provides funds to replace all of the future income that has not yet been earned, and will not be earned, by the breadwinner. In this sense, life insurance guarantees that your family will have the same options in life that you would have wanted to provide for them if the breadwinner—be that you or your spouse, or both— were still there.

The second purpose of life insurance is to aid in properly consuming an estate. The importance of this is lost on most people, primarily because it is misunderstood. I am going to clear up this confusion and delve deeper into the topic in a later chapter, when we discuss exit strategies.

The third purpose of life insurance is to transfer an estate. This will also be further discussed in a later chapter, when we talk about estate planning. For now, it's important to know that life insurance will protect your precious, as well as aid in other important transitions down the line.

As far as types of life insurance go and how they all really work—I would need another book just for that.

Life insurance is an area misunderstood by most people, as they haven't had the time or wherewithal to fully analyze the different policies available. Selecting policies must be done on a case-by-case basis, and should take into account your entire financial situation.

The right type and amount of life insurance cannot be discussed or calculated in a vacuum. A proper plan takes everything into account.

The goal is to employ life insurance policies that can satisfy all three purposes previously mentioned. However, most life insurance products cannot do this. The right advisor or financial expert can help you find a policy that will cover all of these needs and suit your own specific purposes.

So now that you know *why* you need coverage, how do you know *how much* coverage you should have?

How much is the "right" amount?

If I had a dollar for every time I've been asked this question in my thirty years of financial service, I'd be on my own private island sipping piña coladas and enjoying the sunshine.

The fact is, there are countless generic methods and random formulas that are supposed to tell you how much life insurance you need to protect your family. None of them take into account anything about your specific situation. Who depends on you for financial support, and for how much? What colleges might your sons or daughters want to attend? Do you have a special needs child or is there some kind of charitable cause you would like to contribute to and support? All of these are important considerations when it comes to how much life insurance you need.

There are so many variables that should be considered in order to arrive at the correct amount of life insurance to protect and provide for your family. The calculations simply cannot be done by filling in a few blanks and clicking a button.

Unquestionably, none of those one-size-fits-all calculators could possibly provide the correct amount of life insurance for your family.

Imagine if someone were to call into a business radio or TV show and ask how much they should pay for a competitor's business. What could the talk show host do, but give an approximation? He would answer without knowing any of the variables, such as gross sales or net profit, and as a result, that advice could prove to be incredibly damaging, should the caller choose to follow it.

This is a hypothetical situation; in reality, no one in their right mind should, or would, make an important business decision without knowing all of the variables and how they factor into their ultimate choice. Yet, this hypothetical situation regularly plays out in the life insurance market. Many people choose life insurance based on generic, rather than personally-tailored, information.

When it comes to your finances, never settle for anything less than the real deal. Get the personalized analysis and discussions that your family needs and deserves.

All of this being said, there are a few broad guidelines that can assist some financial planners in the process. To give you a general idea, the ideal amount of life insurance equates to a full replacement value for all of the income that the breadwinner would have earned over his or her lifetime. You want money to be there for any number of unaccounted emergencies and unforeseen events that can occur in life. They might occur with you or without you, and to have the cushion of life insurance could mean a lot to your family.

Remember our definition of insurance: replacement value. This applies to life insurance as well, and is called Human Life Value (HLV). HLV is the economic term used to describe the full economic replacement of a person's lost income. *This* is the perfect amount of life insurance to have, at a bare minimum. It will fully replace all of the income a breadwinner would have earned.

The bare minimum amount of life insurance should represent enough insurance to replace the current net income that would be discontinued if one of the breadwinners were to pass away.

We also recommend discussing a midpoint of 50 percent of HLV. That is usually a good start to bridging those gaps that so many people seem to have. Please see the worksheet for more guidance.

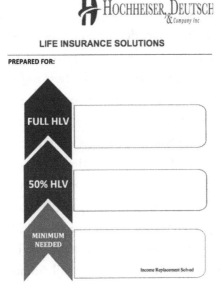

When it comes to disability insurance, the appropriate measurement is to cover as much of your net after-tax income as possible. Essentially, you need to cover all of your lifestyle costs: your mortgages, other household expenses, school costs, food, utilities, cars, etc. The proper amount of combined life and disability insurance helps provide your family with economic confidence about their future. Why wouldn't you want that for your family?

I advocate that the goal is always to have maximum insurance at a minimum cost. However, that doesn't always mean writing the smallest check. In all aspects of these protection components, I favor having very large coverage amounts with high deductibles. You generally don't want to trade small dollars with the insurance companies because when you do that, the insurance companies usually win and you usually lose.

Now, let's say you do take my suggestion and get life insurance. The next question asked is always: who will be the beneficiary? If the client doesn't know estate planning, he'll always say, "I guess it goes to my wife, and then the kids." If the husband and wife die, the children will see the money at age eighteen—typically an age too young to handle the money. Therefore, your will and your insurance need to be coordinated so that what happens to the money is in line with your actual wishes. Seven or eight times out of ten, wills and life insurance are not set up correctly. The attorneys might draft a great will, but they don't circle back to the insurance to make sure it's coordinated with that will. Meanwhile, the insurance person was just selling insurance and has no idea that the product isn't coordinated with the will. Somebody has to be in charge. Somebody has to make sure this vital coordination between the wills and life insurance doesn't fall through the cracks.

There are so many things in life that we have no control over. We cannot do anything to prevent them from occurring. However, there are many things we can control and prepare for just in case. Coordinating your life insurance and your will is one of those things you can control.

This brings me to the next critical step of protecting the precious: having up-to-date wills and trusts. This is an area of much procrastination and delay. I get it—it's hard to have that discussion with your family. Both you and your spouse have to agree on who will be the guardians, who should be the trustees, who should be the executors. *Guardians, trustees, and executors...* more like *lions and tigers and bears—oh my!*

Writing your will can definitely be a daunting task. But in the absence of a will, how will your estate be managed in the event of your death? If a will is not in place and up-to-date, your children may not be protected and provided for.

Your family is the most important thing to you in the whole world; please don't put this off any longer.

You can do all of the planning and have all the pensions, investments, and insurance you like, but if you don't have a will, then what happens after you are gone is left to chance. You're working every day to build a better future for you and your family. Yet if you and your spouse passed away without a will, your children would be in trouble.

While I am not an attorney, I have worked with many clients during this process of planning a will. From my experience, I recommend the following guidelines when drafting your will:

- Pick guardians who will love your children as their own, possibly someone who is currently a father or mother figure. Try to take into account the geography of where they live and where your extended family may be.

- I strongly believe in having a separate trustee to have control over the flow of money, for the simple reason that most people are not good at managing finances. Having checks and balances between guardians and trustees is important.

- I do not endorse children receiving their full inheritance when they turn eighteen. Most eighteen-year-olds I know have no idea how to manage money and make mature decisions. God forbid your teenage son or daughter gets a Ferrari instead of going to college! It seems a far-fetched scenario, but why introduce temptation?

Many people do not develop a fully mature understanding of money until they reach their mid-thirties. Some, unfortunately, never develop that mature understanding. You want your children to have funds for college, life expenses, and other items, but you also want them to use it wisely. Therefore, it makes sense to wait to give them major chunks of their inheritance until they are older, and hopefully able to handle it better. This way, they are more likely to use what you have built and provided in order to secure their future instead of squandering it on mistakes and bad judgment.

The trustees can help your children by monitoring access to their money. You can further organize your children's ability to spend by limiting the distribution of the balance of the funds. You can map it out so that the funds come in pieces as your children hit certain milestones, like at ages twenty-seven, thirty-one, and thirty-three, for example. Your attorney can make proper recommendations on how to best structure the payment schedule.

And that brings me to an important point: please be sure to consult with an estate planning attorney to handle your wills and trusts. This is necessary to ensure that all documents are valid and in line with your best wishes. Don't just consult the attorney who did your house closing. You really need an estate planning specialist handling these most important affairs. It is very important to ensure you have proper coordination among all your protection components. A good advisor should be able to check on all of this for you and provide guidance.

Many people think they have this area covered, when in reality they do not. I've met with many couples who think they have their estate figured out. If either of them were to pass away, they have a minor's trust to protect their children, a separate trustee and guardian, and all supporting documentation. That all seems good, right?

However, upon meeting with many of those couples and reviewing all of their protection components, we often discover that their life insurance and their beneficiary designations aren't coordinated with their wills, just as I mentioned before. That means that if both of them were to pass away, the life insurance proceeds wouldn't go directly to the trust for the children, since they would be minors. The funds would be held up in court, and the courts would then have to appoint a custodian for the funds. The whole process would be anything but smooth and concise.

The correction is relatively simple if you know what you're looking for. You just need to make the contingent beneficiary the minors' trust created through the Will. Problem solved—and potential crisis averted.

I tell you this story to stress the importance of cross-checking all important protection components. A great advisor will align these moving parts for you.

Most people simply don't take care of their wills properly. I had a client whose business sold medical devices. I told him, "Dave, you've got to get this resolved. When can I get an attorney to see you? When can we get it done?"

I reminded him that he had four children and that he worked every day to build a better future for himself and his family. Yet, without a will, if he and his wife were to pass away, if, God forbid, they were in an accident, his family would be in deep trouble. The money would not be handled right. At eighteen, the kids would get all of the funds. They would be young and uneducated, unused to dealing with money. They'd make mistakes, and their whole future could be altered because you didn't have a proper will completed and signed.

Fortunately, he listened, and we were able to get his will properly set up. This is why, in some sense, I feel that my job is a noble calling—I'm making sure that the children of my clients are properly protected, and not just the clients themselves.

I've highlighted the importance of protecting your ability to earn an income. Now let's discuss how to protect that income once it is in the bank.

We currently live in a very litigious society. It is mind-boggling to me that someone could go into a McDonald's, buy hot coffee, get burned, and then sue McDonald's and win. But that's the way the world works. You must therefore be sure you're protected from any liabilities.

Entrepreneurs are very aware of this open-ended liability, as they are often targets of litigation and often get sued. Moreover, nobody sues for just $1 million anymore. Most lawsuits are $5 million, $10 million, or more. That means you need a very large liability umbrella that picks up where your car insurance and homeowners insurance leaves off.

The days of a $1 million umbrella policy being the standard are long over.

Another important part of protecting your assets is ensuring that your business is in order. If you have a company with multiple partners, it is critical to make sure that you have an up-to-date partnership agreement, a buy-sell agreement, and proper funding for the agreement. It's important to address this issue immediately, so that if something happens to you or one of your partners, the business doesn't take a huge financial hit because there is one less partner pulling his or her weight to bring in revenue or helping to run the company.

Often, people don't put their business in proper financial order. I have personally witnessed the broad-reaching effects for all parties involved when this is the case—and let me tell you, it isn't pretty.

You have worked so hard for so long to become an entrepreneur and build your business. It would be a shame to have it all under attack from factors that are out of your control.

A client of mine once introduced me to a man who was one of three business partners. The man wanted to discuss financial planning, a retirement plan, and insurance. As we talked, I asked him questions about his family, his business and all of his protection components. Through this discussion, I discovered that he had no life insurance at all. "Listen," I told him, "you have three children and no life insurance. You really need to put some life insurance in place, both personally and for the business."

He said, "Yeah, but I'm overweight and I have diabetes."

We tried to get him approved for life insurance, but he was declined for his sugar levels and his diabetes. I told him to take care of his diabetes, get his sugar counts under control and then we could try again later. We spoke six months later, and he said his sugar levels were improving.

"Great!" I said. "Let's reapply! It's time to get your family covered." But he put it off instead. Six months later, I checked in again. He said he still wasn't ready, and that he would let me know when he would like to reapply.

He died at 41 years of age. He had a massive heart attack and left his widow and children very little money. The business was a complete disaster because he didn't have any of these agreements established. Consequently, his wife had to engage in a stressful and drawn-out legal battle with the remaining partners in this business—while at the same time having to sell the family house on Long Island and move to North Carolina. I remember standing at the gravesite of the man, distraught for the wife and two young children he left behind. I felt so frustrated because he wouldn't let me help him.

I was upset because what I do for a living should have protected his widow and children from the extreme financial hardship they were about to face. It hurts knowing that I could have prevented so much hardship, if only he had let me. When his wife came to see me to talk about her financial situation, I went through all of her expenses and had to tell her not to get her nails done as often and not to open the pool that year. It was one of the hardest things I have had to do in my career. Who wants to have that kind of conversation?

You want to spare your spouse from having a conversation like that with someone like me. It's just too selfish not to think about it. This woman could have kept her home and her lifestyle if her husband had addressed these issues before he died. So many people put it off—perhaps because it's not fun to deal with, perhaps because they feel invincible. They feel they won't get sick or disable or die, so they don't have the right protection. "It happens to others, not me," they may think.

We hope they're right, but what if they are not?

Figuring out how to combine the various protection components may seem a fine tightrope to walk, but I assure you, once you have the best combinations of protection components in place, you will feel safer than having your feet on solid ground. The right protection components will ease you through the most difficult obstacles in life and ensure your lifestyle, your assets, and your family's finances will never be dramatically impacted by unexpected life changes. So protect the precious and get your protection components in perfect order.

Spotlight: LTC

Long-term care insurance has become part of many financial discussions lately. In many cases, it is in one's best interest to provide for the expense of possibly needing long term care assistance, either at home or at a facility, later in life. Why? Because the cost for care has become astronomical. But the old solution—buying long-term care insurance—simply does not cut it anymore.

Years ago, those who were concerned about such potential expenses bought long-term care insurance in order to feel at ease about their future. Years later, there are now major issues with the cost of these policies. Between being in a prolonged low interest rate environment and the fact that the actuaries now realize that they miscalculated the claims, premium rates for existing long-term care policies have started to increase—big time.

Premium increases at 40-50 percent, or even 60 percent, have recently occurred. Now those who thought they put their concerns to rest have grave concerns about whether or not to keep their policy. No one really knows what their total cost for these policies will come to in the end.

At the same time, new innovations that have developed over the last few years can assist those who find themselves in such a precarious situation. The answer is to couple whole life insurance policies with long-term care riders.

This pairing offers a lot of flexibility in how you choose to utilize benefits down the road when you're older and retired. Now is a more strategic time to make such decisions, as at that point you will have much more clarity on what resources you may need and those you will not need.

Whole life policies with the long-term care riders offer multiple ways you can use the policy, and it's not a use-it-or-lose-it situation. In fact, it can also be made a part of your estate planning and removed from your taxable estate if you so wish.

It's definitely worth the investigation. I recently designed a phenomenal plan involving a ten-pay whole life policy where the policy is guaranteed to be paid up in ten years, even without the dividends, and that included the long-term care option. Many of our entrepreneur clients love the idea of being done funding some plans after ten years.

The key is to have a design that fits your situation and that gives you a multitude of options later on.

Chapter 4

The Four Financial Stages of Your Life

Some see life as a roulette wheel that just keeps on spinning. If you're lucky, the roulette ball lands on your number and you hit the jackpot. On the other hand, if lady fortune is not in your favor, you can bet it all and lose big. Regardless of the outcome, the game continues.

I view life—or more specifically, your financial life—like a game of foursquare, with four distinct stages we all go through. But in this game of foursquare, there is no back and forth or up and down. Instead, you only move forward as you build your wealth and become wiser about managing your money—or not.

Most people who are reading this book are probably in Stage Two, Stage Three or possibly retired and in Stage Four. Use this chapter as a way to benchmark your progress and gauge where you're going. Whatever stage you're in, the pro-active work you do along the way will pay dividends down the road.

Stage 1

Just The Beginning: Your Career, Your Family, and Your Finances

In stage one, the focus is on family protection and income replacement in the event you became sick or hurt and unable to work. Some needs to address at this stage include covering household and lifestyle expenses, growing college funds, and planning financial security for the wealth you will accumulate in the future.

The proper amounts of disability insurance benefits and life insurance are critical to the family at this point, as is having proper wills and estate planning documents in place. Your family (if you have one at this point), is young and would be severely affected if these items were not complete. So, protect the precious, as we discussed in the previous chapter.

This is the best time to establish good habits. "Good habits" means having security and protection in order, as well as establishing a savings routine. Developing good saving habits now puts you on the path for a solid future.

Stage 2

Starting To Cook: Developing Your Career and Your Earnings

At Stage Two, you have begun to accumulate wealth and savings and are now earning more money. Accordingly, your lifestyle has also increased in both cost and enjoyment. You enjoy nicer cars, vacations, and the prospects for your future lifestyle are good. Hopefully, the future only gets bigger and brighter from here on out.

Protection for both income replacement and family security needs has not decreased since Stage One. Rather, your need for protection has increased concurrently with your higher level of success. With your increased earnings, you also face increased taxes. It's time to start planning and strategizing to make the most of your income at tax time.

Additionally, as you have started to accumulate wealth in various accounts, the need to protect your assets from lawsuits has become more important. Paying proper attention to *where* you are building wealth also becomes more important. A good financial advisor will help ensure that you are properly setting yourself up for retirement and working successfully towards achieving important goals and dreams.

Stage 3

Bringing It to a Boil: The Establishment Phase of Your Career

You've built a nice life for yourself and your family. You have a thriving business, maybe various real estate holdings, too. You are thoroughly enjoying the financial resources you have built. Welcome to Stage Three.

Now that you've put in the effort, you are looking forward to the prospect of not having to work for much longer. Thoughts of financial freedom have begun to enter your mind, and you have begun training your eye on retirement, or at least on slowing down a little in the next five to fifteen years.

Most of the original protection elements are still vital, but a new consideration at this stage is protecting your assets in the event you need long-term care assistance or facilities. You are also starting to have thoughts about leaving a legacy in line with your feelings and wishes for your heirs, and you may have an idea about who else you would potentially like to help with your legacy.

Taxes play an even greater role in this stage, and the pain of having to pay them is all too real. This is the time to map out strategies for how you might manage what you have built with the least amount of tax erosion. The ideal situation is to maximize your net income in retirement without losing sight of creative ways to keep some funds flexible so that you have the ability to help your children and eventual grandchildren.

Stage 4

Letting It Simmer: Enjoying Your Retirement Years:

You are now focused on your life in retirement. It's all about having fun, deciding when and where you're going to travel, and seeing the children and grandchildren as much as possible. Life is filled with new experiences: graduations, recitals, and other milestones.

You enjoy being able to assist your family financially when you think they could use some help, but are maybe too afraid to ask. You want to be able to use all the wealth you created to get the most out of your life now, and share that with the family as well.

And when you are gone, you want your children and grandchildren to have as much financial security as possible, even though you won't be there to help guide them. They may make some financial mistakes along the way, but it may be possible for you to bail them out while not detracting from the lifestyle you enjoyed.

The journey through each of these four stages is very important. Most entrepreneurs agree that the ideal final destination is to be able to afford to retire as early and as comfortably as possible, even if you choose to keep working because you want to.

In other words, the goal in this game of foursquare is financial freedom.

Financial freedom means different things to different people. Financial freedom for one entrepreneur might mean that when they turn fifty-five, they can afford to retire, but can choose instead to work at a slower pace. Maybe they adjust their schedule and take on fewer customers, or maybe they only work a few days a week. They have the luxury of making those decisions without financial pressure. For another entrepreneur, financial freedom might mean being able to leave the business at sixty and move to their vacation home by the beach.

The bottom line is that financial freedom means having the liberty to choose—being able to do what you want, when you want!

But financial freedom doesn't have to be an end goal. In fact, with proper planning and coordination, financial freedom can be attained—and maintained—throughout your journey.

The beauty of financial freedom is that work becomes more enjoyable, because you have the option to wake up one day and say, "I'm done! I don't want to do this anymore!" and leave it at that. You have the financial resources behind you to take care of yourself and your family, no matter what you choose to do.

So how do you navigate the stages and maximize your financial potential?

Planning is one component, but the real challenge is to really see the complete picture. When someone comes to me at forty years old, I'm not only trying to help them accumulate money for the different things they want at forty. I'm trying to put them in a position so that, by virtue of what we do when they are forty or fifty, they can live a better life in their sixties, seventies, and eighties.

I'm looking beyond their current phase, and into the future— something not many financial planners do. How you build wealth now, in what order, and with what investment products has a big influence on with how much you'll pay in taxes and how you'll be able to access your wealth later. So at every stage, you must be thinking about the next one. A good, proactive advisor can help you create financial freedom for you and for your family.

Chapter 5

The Mortgage Opportunity Cost

L et's talk mortgages.

Do you suddenly have the urge to pull out your hair? I don't blame you. Talking about mortgages is like scheduling a check-up with the doctor. We all know we should go in regularly for an annual exam to monitor our health, but who actually does, and who actually wants to? We seem to think of the doctor like an inevitable bearer of bad news, one we should avoid at all costs. And yet, health affects our lives in a very profound way.

The same is true of your mortgage.

What kind of mortgage you have—or whether or not you have one—affects how much money you spend or save over your lifetime.

You don't need to be a mortgage expert, but if you want to save yourself from losing money, there are a few things you should know. So in this chapter, I'm going to take you through the mortgage rapid round.

Mortgages are very misunderstood financial instruments, both in our society as a whole and among many successful entrepreneurs. Years ago, mortgage rates were averaging 12 percent, 13 percent, and even 14 percent. It was a horrible time for real estate buyers to have a mortgage because it cost so much money to finance a home. Fortunately, the economics today are very different. Interest rates have been at historic lows, and as we will be discussing later in the book, income tax rates are more favorable now, too.

The modern economy favors home ownership and mortgages more than in previous economies. Still, I find many entrepreneurs don't choose the best way to finance either their primary home or a vacation home.

Plenty of people and resources will tell you what you need to know about mortgages. But here again, those people and resources often don't give all of the economic variables and items to consider when making these extremely important decisions. Typically, they will tell how much interest you will pay and how much interest you'll save if you pay down or pay off your mortgage. What these sources fail to relay is the difference in tax savings, the financial benefits, or possible use of the money between various mortgages and methods of payment.

I've touched on the importance of tax planning at every stage of life, and mortgage has a huge impact on this area. Yet the "experts" never really mention this aspect of a mortgage – and they are wrong, wrong, wrong not to do so.

What about the chance that your cash flow might change?

What about the fact that money not spent on the mortgage can be saved or invested?

What about making interest and growing that saved money? How are the "experts" discussing and calculating that?

Quite simply, no one is looking at the big picture. No one is calculating the real net cost. Most importantly, no one is considering the opportunity cost that comes with having too much money tied up in your house.

If your company makes a six percent profit, and you invest it back into your business and then make a fourteen percent profit the next quarter, that's a good deal. That's efficient use of capital based on today's economics.

When you break down the mortgage puzzle, it's really the same song and dance. It's all about the actual cost, which is not what it appears to be on the surface. Breaking down that cost is the tricky part.

Let's say that three siblings all buy identical homes, worth $1 million, each located in the same affluent neighborhood. One brother, Sam, pays for his up front with cash. He has no mortgage and he's thrilled. The sister, Diane, pays for half up front and has a fifteen-year mortgage on the rest. The youngest brother, Rick, buys the third house, puts down twenty percent, and gets a thirty-year mortgage.

A few months later, they have a barbecue at Sam's house. He's making steaks and serving up sympathy about how sorry he is that his siblings are paying all this interest—hundreds of thousands in interest, he estimates.

Little does Sam know, he's the one who should be crying.

Hypothetically, in twenty years their homes will all be worth $2 million, no matter how they financed them. They're all worth the same by virtue of where they are; it has nothing to do with how they paid for it. What does change is *how much* they each paid for it. And Sam's got it all wrong.

Let's look at Sam first. All of the $1 million that he put down did nothing for the value of his house. That money would have done as much good for him if he had buried it in the basement instead. Because his home's value went from $1 million to $2 million, he lost the opportunity to make interest on that additional $1 million in gained value.

Diane, who put down half and did a fifteen-year mortgage, does indeed pay interest, but she also benefits from a nice tax deduction due to that interest. Unfortunately, like Sam, she lost out on that chunk of change she used as a down payment. However, when it's all added up—including what she could have made on her money, plus principal and interest—a surprising conclusion is revealed: she ultimately paid less than Sam for the value of her house.

Which brings us to Rick. In this example, the money that Rick didn't put down (or bury in the basement) was invested and made four percent compound interest. Additionally, he garnered tax deductions and savings on the mortgage he was paying. Those gains were all reinvested at a certain amount of interest. Side by side, Rick, who everyone thought would be paying up the nose in interest rates on his thirty-year mortgage, actually pays the lowest net cost to own the house for that same time period.

If I were to walk these siblings through the same process I do with my clients and project the costs and deductions for each method of payment, you would see that Sam paid $2 million, Diane paid maybe $1.8 million, and Rick was in the ballpark of $1.3 million. That amounts to hundreds of thousands of dollars saved—or lost—depending on how each sibling managed their money. As you can see, the mortgage game is counterintuitive, which is why so many entrepreneurs today are losing significant amounts when they could be saving—and gaining.

Moreover, mortgage decisions don't just affect how much you save; they also determine how resilient you will be in uncertain times. Can you withstand loss of income or other unexpected events? The way you structure your mortgage could be the determining factor in this.

Let's look at another couple, John and Jane Smith. Back in 2002, John and Jane bought the house of their dreams for $1.5 million. They put down $500,000 and then took out a $1 million mortgage. They opted for the 15-year mortgage instead of the 30-year mortgage because the rate was a little lower, and that way, they would pay off the house sooner. The bank also recommended pre-paying the mortgage to reduce it even more and save tons of money on interest.

John and Jane did just as they were instructed to do. They pre-paid $1500 every month toward reducing their mortgage because they were told it was the smart choice, and the Smiths were a smart couple.

In 2002, they were paying 5 percent interest for the mortgage. Things were good for a number of years—until 2008 hit. The financial crisis was felt around the world, and especially in the North American real estate market. By 2009, John's income had decreased dramatically. His business was not earning the same money as it had been. Suddenly, John and Jane were struggling to pay their bills and make the mortgage. They needed help, so they went to the bank.

"We have been really good borrowers," they said. "We have never missed a mortgage payment and we have been pre-paying our mortgage every month. We bought our house for $1.5 million and now we only owe $600,000. We're not making the money we were and we need to take some money back out of the house to help cover expenses."

The bank looked at their current income and offered a polite, but firm, "Sorry, Charlie." They couldn't offer a re-financing deal. John and Jane's income was not high enough to qualify for a mortgage under the current guidelines.

In 2009, the banks were not lending money, even if you had great credit. Foreclosures were happening left and right, and lending was tight. It didn't matter if you were disabled or making less money; they were not helping you out. On the contrary, you would be considered a big risk.

So now picture John and Jane: They couldn't afford their payments, and all of their money had been virtually trapped in their house. They couldn't get a loan to retrieve some of that money from out of the house. What were they going to do?

The only way to get money out of their house now was to sell it and to uproot their family. However, the dream house they had bought for $1.5 million was now worth around $950,000. Remember, the housing crisis dramatically affected all real estate valuations. This is also assuming the Smiths could even sell the house, and that the person they were selling to could get their own mortgage.

Stay in the house and sink into a larger amount of debt, or sell the house for $950,000 and lose more than $500,000? It's a terrible situation, but it is what the Smiths were facing.

How could they have avoided this mess?

Again, it's counterintuitive, but by running the numbers and looking into the future, you'll see how much you can help yourself, and your family, by going against the grain.

Here is what I would have advised the Smiths to do: take out a 30-year mortgage, even one with a little higher interest rate, and don't pre-pay the extra $1,500 a month. Instead put the $1,500 monthly into a very safe, low-risk account. Now they would get a larger tax deduction, because by having a 30-year mortgage and not pre-paying it, they preserved their tax deductions and would have had a better foundation for weathering the 2008 recession, as I'll explain shortly.

It's a paradox; most entrepreneurs desperately want more tax deductions, and yet many times, they prepay and pay down mortgages where they would otherwise have a tax deduction. Doesn't quite make sense, does it?

If you're not paying attention to how much you'll pay in taxes when you cash out of an investment, you're not getting the whole picture. If your investment advisor isn't sharing this information with you, he's doing you a disservice. Let me show you what I mean.

There will always be taxes that have to be paid. The government's attitude is, "You can pay now or you can pay later, as long as you pay." If you pay the government now— meaning that every year the investment makes money, you pay taxes on it that same year— the money used to pay the taxes has to come from somewhere, right? Either you have to sell off part of the investment, or you have to pay the taxes out of your income from your business that year. If you don't pay taxes now, then you'll ultimately have to pay taxes when you sell the investment. So even if the graph of how well your investment is doing looks like you're going up the side of a mountain, higher and higher, that mountain is actually hollowed out! You own part of the mountain, but the government owns the rest.

A very important caveat: If you or your spouse spends the difference in your payments instead of saving, then you will not be better off. If someone goes from a 15-year mortgage to a 30-year mortgage and spends the difference of the payments rather than putting it away—if they don't have the discipline, or they haven't implemented the automated savings I mentioned earlier in the book—then they would be better off doing a 15-year mortgage.

If the Smiths had followed this program of having a the 30-year mortgage, and had the discipline to save and invest, then they would have had approximately $400,000 in their account as a cushion when 2008 hit. They could have afforded to stay in their house, at least for a while, and not uproot their family or sell the house at such a big loss. They would have had time on their side, with the luxury of waiting out that horrible financial storm.

Quite a different picture, isn't it?

In Chapter 3, I wrote that you must always protect against the unexpected. In order to protect your mortgage, you have to look at the economics of where we are today.

Currently, you can get a mortgage for 4-5 percent, and you can deduct that mortgage interest from your taxes. Once you factor in that deduction, it costs you 2.5-3 percent—that is your real cost. If you have money already invested and earning more than that, do you really want to cash out that investment to put down more money on your house?

You control the money. Keep it that way.

If you can develop an automated organized plan of saving, you are better off saving the difference and putting it away. This means greater tax deductions, more access to the money, and more choices under your control, rather than controlled by banks.

When you pay and prepay your mortgage, the bank takes that money, and then they loan it to someone else—for a credit card at 20 percent or a car loan at 5 percent or 6percent. The banks create a "velocity of money" with the funds they receive. That is how they make money: by using other people's money—your money. They don't produce or manufacture hard goods. It is all about velocity of money: moving cash flows around to constantly make money on the turn of capital.

So when you take out a mortgage, are you using other people's money? Or are they using yours?

Much of the generic financial advisement out there is for the average person in this country, not for you, the successful entrepreneur. Some of that generic advice may still be helpful, but some of it may be extremely harmful. The mortgage situation is just one example of how generic advice can cause tremendous financial harm. I've helped many entrepreneurs create more wealth or lower their real costs of buying real estate, with the same cash flow and assets, just by using their mortgages effectively. The difference could be hundreds of thousands of dollars or more over a 20-year period just by doing things the efficient way.

You hold the cards. You can control what you want to do, and if your life changes, you have the ability to weather those changes by getting smart with your mortgage.

Chapter 6

Taxability Costs:
The Good, The Bad,
And The Ugly

R emember in Chapter 2 when we talked about your savings habits? Well, once you are saving that 15-20 percent of your gross income, the question becomes, where should you put it? You want to build wealth and you also want to protect that wealth by making sure the financial strategies you are employing are tax-efficient and not, in fact, costing you more money. This leads us to the big question:

How much money really goes out for taxes, and what's really in it for you?

We have been brainwashed as a society to adore and worship "the miracle of compound interest." Compound interest does seem like a great thing, but what about the compounding of lost tax dollars that comes with it?

Compounded lost tax dollars and the lost interest you would have made with those dollars are the nightmare that no one is talking about. When compounded lost tax dollars are calculated and measured, almost everyone is startled—and then horrified.

What exactly do I mean when I refer to compounded lost tax dollars?

Most likely, you've invested money before. For instance, if you put $100,000 into an investment, an advisor who helps you with that investment would show you a compounding interest chart, which usually resembles a mountain. The compounding interest chart shows how much money you would make on your investment over time, which depends on factors such as the rise and fall of the market and the compounding growth of the initial investment. It would show, for instance, that your $100,000 investment could triple in twenty years.

The chart is a great tool, but it is not without flaws. Crucially, what the chart does not show you is what effect Uncle Sam has on the gains and losses of what you make and put away.

For instance, in year two of investing, let's say you had a $2,000 gain. That $2,000 gain comes with a $700 tax. And when your accountant says you have to write a $700 check to pay for that gain, you don't call up UBS or E-trade and sell $700 worth of that fund to pay the tax. Instead, you write a check. You take $700 out of another account, and pay your tax—and that money never gets measured or accounted for. Your investment is still compounding, and it's looking great, but the $700 you sent to the IRS is lost forever—along with all the future interest that you would have made on that $700.

Because the truth is, you didn't just lose $700. In order to figure out what you really lost, you have to compound your $700 in taxes for that one year by a reasonable rate of interest every year until you die, or, for the sake of this example, until you retire. All in all, if you use a 3 percent interest rate, that compounded number comes to roughly $12,000—no small amount!

The second year of investing, your accountant informs you that you made $3,800, and now have to pay $1,450 in taxes. Once again, you write a check, and the cycle continues.

Do you see how we have all been led astray? Advisors in the financial world have been showing people the miracle of these "mountain charts" of money, which only show the good. They don't show the bad, and they certainly don't show you the ugly. But I'm not afraid to say it: When it comes to investing, the bad is the taxes, and the ugly is the compounding of those lost tax dollars that you no longer have the ability to invest.

If your business grosses $1 million, then you're going to have a party. But if your overhead was $999,000, you didn't really make any money. The same idea applies to your savings and investments. Our world is completely focused on rate of return and growth. Nobody measures the consequences of the taxability of an investment, nor where those tax dollars are coming from every year. And so we end up losing over time—and losing big, leaving most people wondering why they haven't accumulated more money.

Most entrepreneurs have never been offered to analyze their financial strategies from an after-tax perspective, even though that is the real world. A true look at your portfolio accounts for everything, telling you what you keep *after* all the taxes, fees, and everything else that dilutes your "real gain."

What do you really have left? And what is your strategy really helping you gain?

The amount of wealth in compounded lost tax dollars lost through tax-inefficient strategies is mind boggling. When you compute how much money is lost over time, it is enough to make you sick to your stomach.

As a society, we have also over-glorified high-risk, high-yielding, and high-tax investments. When we compare them to low-risk, low-tax investments, we somehow forget all the risk and taxes.

Unfortunately, in real life, it doesn't really work that way.

Math is not money and money is not math.

Imagine going to a fruit stand and buying five oranges. You bring them home, put them on your windowsill, and walk away. You "set 'em and forget 'em," so to speak. Then you leave for a month-long vacation in Hawaii. What do those five oranges look like when you return? They're disgusting! They're finished. Let's say, of those five oranges, you eat two and then you go on vacation. In this case, three oranges will decompose.

Now, instead of the oranges, imagine it's your money on the windowsill. Just as the oranges wrinkle and decay in the sun, so too does your money decay over time. Factors like inflation and taxes cause money to erode or dissipate, just like those oranges. In math, two plus two equals four, but that's not always the case with your money.

People assume math and money are the same thing—but they're not. Math is math. It stays put. Money, on the other hand, is more of a living, breathing, fungible, depreciative, diminishing potential asset. Math is constant. Money is not constant because various factors erode money all the time. Some of them you see and know about, such as inflation; some of them, like taxes, are more insidious.

In addition to taxes, you also have to take risk into account. You have to assess your ability to handle the ups and downs of your investment, and how you can stay in it for the long haul. This is important not only for you to be able to grow your money, but also to avoid triggering possible taxable gains from previous years that are not yet realized.

The next huge factor in managing taxes is how you are going to use the money later on. How are you going to access it and what are the efficiencies or inefficiencies with that process? What happens later?

Years ago, Steven Covey wrote a highly acclaimed book called *The Seven Habits of Highly Effective People*, where he stated the following:

"You begin with the end in mind."

When it comes to financial planning and financial strategies, you have to look down the road to see how you are going to access your money in the future, and what the negative ramifications might be. You don't want to focus solely on dollars on a page. You want to know how much of those funds are really going to be available to use after taxes.

Many entrepreneurs and their CPAs are fans of setting up pension and profit-sharing plans to build wealth and get much-needed current tax deductions. These types of qualified retirement plans are great tools for this purpose. However, not all retirement plans are designed equally. The goal is to custom-design a plan, or the right combination of plans, to maximize your deductions and minimize the part of the contribution that has to go to your employees.

The importance of having an efficient retirement plan design cannot be overstated.

We see so many plans in which the business is giving too much to the employees, making the entrepreneur's costs much higher than they need to be. Other times, the plan is not designed to allow the entrepreneur to take full advantage of current pension laws and enjoy a larger deductible contribution. This is, of course, a moving target and needs to be reviewed properly every year to see if there might be a better, more efficient design to serve the entrepreneurs. There is no room here for cookie-cutter designs.

Your employee demographics may change. Incomes may change. And more often than not, plan improvements can be made if someone is really on top of your plan, year in and year out. For instance, as 401(k)s have become commonplace, so have the many levels of fees associated with them. Some 401(k) platforms are just way too expensive. Be sure you have a plan with many options, plenty of fiduciary protection, and a reasonable fee structure. Fees vary widely, so we shop the 401(k) landscape routinely to find the best overall experience that can be had at the lowest possible fees.

Pensions, profit-sharing and 401(k)-type plans are misleading on a personal finance level as well. When your pension or 401(k) investment statement says you have $1 million in your plan, that is not quite true. That $1 million is not really all yours, because if you want to take that money out, it would become 100 percent taxable. Depending on your combined federal, state, and possibly local tax bracket, the government might want as much as 40-45 percent of it. The minute you take the money, the government says, "Where's mine?" This is the greatest drawback to pension and 401(k) plans—when you finally use the money and enjoy it, it becomes 100 percent taxable.

Moreover, the financial industry has done some damage in this area by saying "You'll be in a lower tax bracket in retirement." You have to read between the lines.

If you are in the bottom 95th percentile of all US household incomes, it is possible you will be in a lower tax bracket in retirement. If you are in the top 1 percent or higher of U.S. household incomes, most likely you will not be a lower tax bracket in retirement, because you are actively building wealth specifically to enjoy later in life. If you structure it right, the wealth you are building will produce the kind of income you need to live well and enjoy the fruits of your labor when you retire.

Let me ask you a question: Where do you think tax rates are headed—up or down? Although I wish they were decreasing, it is pretty apparent that the federal government, along with many state and local municipalities, has no money and will need to raise taxes to pay for much-needed services. Taxes have gone up over the last few years, and while some tax increases are clear and obvious, others may slip under the radar. You won't notice them until you've filed your paperwork and want to know why you owe so much money!

In 2013, the top bracket went up, from 35.0 percent to 39.6 percent. That was obvious. However, the additional surtax of 3.8 percent that may come into play on much of your investment income, as well as dividends to pay for Obamacare, may not have been so obvious. Many knew about it, but by the time tax season rolled around, some had forgotten. After all, it is painful to always remember how much tax you are paying. The government also brought back the 3 percent phase-out of your itemized deductions, as well as the ability to lose the deductions for your dependents. Check with your CPA to see how all of this impacts you specifically, but the bottom line is that we are all paying a lot more taxes these days.

That is why it is all the more important to employ various tax-efficient strategies to protect your capital. Keep an eye on what the real deal is, and measure that against other strategies to see if you're doing the best for yourself and your family.

Some people focus on paying the least amount of taxes today and don't really worry about tomorrow. While I think paying less taxes today is very important, I believe that paying the least amount of taxes over your lifetime—both now and later—is most certainly the ideal to work toward. That's our focus: to balance the euphoria of tax deductions today with the pain of taxes later, versus the pain now for euphoria later. Clearly, a strong balance is the way to go.

You should continually ask yourself, "Am I building money in the best places for my situation?"

I believe the financial industry has totally misled people when it comes to how much money you will need in retirement. For years, some in the industry have said you will only need 70-80 percent of your working income in retirement. Think about it. When you are on vacation from work, don't you tend to spend more money? You may play more golf, eat out more often. You certainly have the time to do more, and doing more costs more money. I am not much of a shopper, but when I am on vacation and I am more relaxed, with extra time on my hands, I find myself shopping. What happens when you shop? You buy stuff. It all adds up to spending more money.

Face it: working prevents you from spending more money because you simply do not have the time. Moreover, all of this great technology—amazing, life-changing gadgets and gizmos—will continue to evolve, and you're going to want to buy them. My parents never dreamed they would be buying cell phones, DVRs, and wireless routers for their house. But they are, and it all costs money. Who knows where technology will go next? Wherever it goes, it's going be cool, you're going to buy it, and it's going to cost money. It's that simple.

Items that you own are also going to wear out and will need to be replaced. You may have grandchildren for whom you want to buy presents. You'll want to take them out and "spoil" them. Who knows what expenses will come up. Whatever they are, you want to make sure you have the funds necessary to continue living comfortably.

Ideally, you would want to be able to leave your business making "x" amount of dollars and walk into retirement making the same amount of money, or maybe even more. To some, this idea seems like a stretch, but with a good financial team, it is absolutely possible.

Financial freedom is not taking a pay cut in retirement when you have more time to spend money.

Financial freedom is also knowing that you have the right strategy to maximize your earnings. Taxes, mortgages, insurance—these are all wince-inducing items to consider. But if you embrace them and confront them, you will be empowered to make the most of your wealth, to live and enjoy your life to the fullest.

Chapter 7
The Three Pools of Money

t's very important to remember that there is a difference between the most effective way to *build* wealth and the most effective way to *distribute* wealth. Quite frankly, they are at odds. When it comes to distribution, it's time to stop thinking about all your money as one single pool or grouping of assets. Instead, I'd like you to think in terms of three distinct pools of money.

Most people know they should diversify their assets among stocks, bonds, treasuries, and all kinds of sub-categories and sub-styles of investing. However, most people do not consider how to diversify their assets in terms of the different ways their money will be taxed at distribution time.

These different "pools of money" have different tax aspects to them. Some are taxed now at ordinary income tax rates, some may be taxed as long-term capital gains, and many investments are taxed as a combination of both, which varies from year to year. Some investments grow tax deferred, meaning you pay tax when you take the money out, and some are tax free at distribution time.

So how are you going to access the wealth that you are building in these three pools of money, and what are the tax effects going to be? In other words, are you building these three pools of money with some kind of balance and order?

The first pool is qualified money. This would include all of your pension plan assets, profit sharing, 401(K), SEP, 403(b) and IRAs. Those funds are fully deductible at the time of contribution. They grow tax deferred, and are fully taxable at ordinary income tax rates at distribution time.

Many people advise leaving these assets for last. Others advise not spending them until you are required to start taking minimum distributions. Their reason is that those assets are taxed—but the tax doesn't go away, no matter when you spend them. These assets are always taxed, and taxed at your ordinary income tax bracket. Remember from our earlier conversation that if you build wealth in order to have a nice life later on, you will most likely *not* be in a lower tax bracket in retirement. In fact, the alternative is very possible, as unfortunate as it sounds. If the government continues to have trouble righting its ship, and you have saved and invested intelligently during your working years, you may end up in a higher tax bracket in retirement.

If you look below at the history of U.S. marginal tax rates from 1913-2014, you will see that in 2014 they were below the average of that 101-year history. Now, they seem to be going up. The average top marginal bracket in this country from 1913-2013 has been around 60 percent. It is currently 39.6 percent. If you look at the federal government, your state government, and all the local municipalities, they don't have enough money to pay for all the social programs, pension liabilities, and everything else that needs to be taken care of. It seems inevitable that tax rates will rise.

How are you going to prepare for the likelihood of higher taxes?

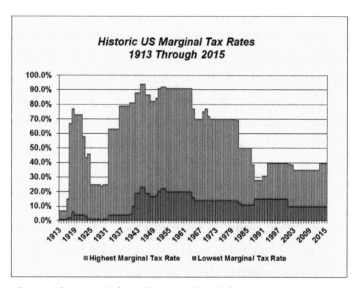

Source: The Living Balance Sheet® (LBS) and the LBS Logo are registered service marks of the Guardian Life Insurance Company of America (Guardian), New York, NY. © Copyright 2005-2016 The Guardian Life Insurance Company of America.

Let's examine what happens as tax rates start to go up again and the top bracket potentially rises significantly. If all your money was in Pool #1 (qualified money), you could be in serious trouble when you retire and start withdrawing those funds to enjoy your life. For example, let's say you had $1 million in Pool #1. If you take out all of that money, you will pay approximately $450,000 in income taxes. Let's say you allow this pool to grow and compound, and it doubles to $2,000,000, while you live on your other pools of money. Just as your money doubles, you will also double your tax by another $450,000. These assets in Pool #1 are taxed as ordinary income on the federal, state, and local level. Currently, you could expect to pay anywhere from a 42-47 percent combined income tax rate. If all of your investments and savings are in Pool #1 and the top tax bracket is up to 70 percent when you retire, you are going to feel some major pain and lose a lot of capital, and you will have nowhere to turn. You may well have put money away when you were in a 39.6 percent, 45.0 percent or 50.0 percent federal tax bracket for a deduction that year. Then, you may be taking it out at 70 percent. I call this reverse tax planning.

The second pool is what we refer to as non-qualified assets. These are after tax investments in stocks, bonds, mutual funds, CDs or bank accounts. These carry with them a combination of long term capital gains taxes (which also went up in 2013) and ordinary income tax rates. Your actual combined overall tax rate on these assets will most likely vary from year to year. For our example here, we will use a combined current blended tax rate of 34 percent that covers federal long term capital gains taxes, state and local taxes. We also have to include the 3.8 percent tax on investment earnings that is paying for Obamacare.

If you had that same $1 million in Pool #2, and you let those assets compound and double over time while you spend your Pool #1 assets, you will also increase your taxes. However, if we are using a 34 percent combined rate, you would have added approximately $340,000 of additional tax over time, rather than the $450,000 as in Pool #1. While this example is very general, it is meant to highlight huge differences that should not be ignored.

The third pool is comprised of tax-free assets, including Roth IRAs and the cash value of most life insurance policies. If utilized correctly, these assets can be accessed on a tax-free basis. You can withdraw income, have access to the cash values of whole life[3] policies, and enjoy the money—all without paying taxes.

Another purpose of whole life policies can be to own a safe, risk-averse cash asset that is not correlated to the stock market.

Some view whole life insurance cash value as similar to municipal bonds without the interest rate risk, but with the main

---

3   Whole life insurance is intended to provide benefit protection for an individual's entire life. With payment of the required guaranteed premiums, you will receive a guaranteed death benefit and guaranteed cash values inside the policy. Guarantees are based on the claims-paying ability of the issuing insurance company. Dividends are not guaranteed and are declared annually by the issuing company's board of directors. Any loans or withdrawals reduced the policy's death benefits and cash values, and affect the policy's dividend and guarantees. Whole life insurance should be considered for its long term value. Early cash value accumulation and early payment of dividends depend upon policy type and/or policy design, and cash value accumulation is offset by insurance and company expenses.

features of a death benefit in retirement and a disability waiver of premium option.[4]

If you build up significant cash value during a stock market decline, you'll be thankful for your cash value in your whole life policy.

There may also be periods of time when your stock market investments are dramatically outperforming your cash value.

The great thing about having both is balance. Should you desire to withdraw funds at a point when the stock market is down, you can access your whole life insurance cash value.

There might be a point when your income tax rates skyrocket—then you can access your whole life cash value with no income taxes provided the policy distribution is structured properly.

Life is all about balance—and having a balance with a multitude of options is always good.

So, let's say that you had $1 million in Pool #3 and let this money double over time while you spent Pool #1 or Pool #2. You would have accumulated $2 million and not have incurred any additional tax. If you let these assets in Pool #3 grow and compound, they will, in most cases, do this without incurring any additional taxes when you eventually use the funds.

In the long run, you want the assets with the least amount of taxes to have the longest compounding curve.

So you would want to start Pool #3 first, and spend it last.

Please understand that this example is meant as a simplified way of looking at what may happen when you use the money

---

4   Riders may incur either additional cost or premium. Rider benefits may not be available in all states.

you are building and start taking income or distributions. Your tax rates, now and in the future, need to be carefully analyzed before an effective distribution plan can be properly designed and implemented. There are many variables and factors that will affect these decisions.

Everybody is focused on Pool #1, which gives you immediate tax savings. When this happens, the advisor looks like a hero. To me, Pool #1 represents euphoria *now*—immediate gratification with serious tax deductions and tax savings—but it means pain *later*.

Pool #2 is a little bit of everything. There are no deductions, but you get some long-term capital gains treatment, and you take advantage of capital losses. It's okay now, and it's okay later.

Pool #3, by contrast, is paying now. There are no deductions, and you may find yourself sitting there saying, "When is my money going to grow?" However, when you take the money out of Pool #3 in retirement, it is totally tax-free. That's when the euphoria kicks in! That's when you're having a party! Every year of your retirement you get money, and you don't have to pay income tax on it. That's the best. Pool #3 is pain initially, and no, it is not exciting right out of the gate. But it is euphoria later, and it is absolutely worth it.

It's euphoria later, when you're likely not working or earning additional income.

It's euphoria later when you're older and probably don't want to risk your assets or your retirement (or both).

It's euphoria later when you really want things to be easy, and you don't want to have worries or stress.

It's euphoria later when you hope to be able to sit back and relax.

To me, Pool #3 is euphoria *later*, when you can really appreciate it *most*.

Now, you're an entrepreneur. You pay estimates. You file your taxes on April 15th. On April 16th, you go back to work, to make more money and help you regain what you lost. When you retire, though, you'll most likely never again have to go back to work on April 16th to make back the money you paid in taxes. That's why I say that you have to find a balance between happiness now and paying later, and paying now and happiness later. The balance is critical.

Personally, I find that Pools #1 and #3 are the most powerful. Both have elements of pain and euphoria. They also both have a huge effect on building wealth. But remember: both need to be kept *carefully* balanced.

Another important consideration in this discussion is whether to spend the most risk-based assets first in retirement, in addition to the highest taxed assets. This comes from a perspective of having the most security later in life when you might not deal with risk as well, or when you may not have the tolerance for it.

In all of this, I am not minimizing the power of tax deferral, or even more importantly the emotional desire to save and see progress. I think it is very important to realize that many things in life are based on momentum. Entrepreneurs are motivated to move money into retirement plans as quickly as possible. They are saving a lot of money on current income taxes. Instead of sending money to the IRS, they put their money into an account with their name on it. That is a very good feeling. That good feeling motivates you to save more, and the whole thing keeps propelling you to accumulate more money. That's all good, since some entrepreneurs do not save enough. You just want to be aware of what is going to happen later on, so you can try to build wealth with a good balance between your pools.

So how are you building your pools? Do you have a good balance?

It's definitely better to measure and address how you are building your pools as early in life as possible. There are still some strategies you can use to address this later in life if you find yourself out of balance or too exposed in any one taxable area. Different methodologies yield very different results over time. There are a lot of moving parts when it comes to setting yourself up for having options in retirement. This is where you need someone looking after the big picture, someone who will coordinate all financial strategies, products, and advisors—a quarterback, if you will. You lose out if you don't have someone looking at the bigger picture and considering what's going to happen down the road.

So what's your plan?

As I mentioned earlier, coordination between protection components is important. Coordination between wealth-building and wealth-distributing strategies is extremely critical, because you want to build wealth in the best proportion in the different pools and use them at the right times later. This requires total coordination and a holistic understanding of the economics of your situation, in order to determine how to best use what you have built in the most efficient order.

Employing different methods of distributing these pools of money at different times will *definitely* yield different results. The difference in amounts of taxes paid and income received can be quite substantial throughout your lifetime.

Chapter 8

Look for the Exits
Before You Enter

G

ood planning means thinking ahead and building in different options for what I call "exit strategies" in retirement. There are a few different ways to utilize your three different pools to engineer tax deductions in retirement. This is very exciting because when you are retired, you may no longer have any methods of getting tax deductions.

When you're running your business there are many types of tax deductions you might be getting. When you're retired, your children are not dependents anymore, your mortgage may be paid off, and if you're done with your business, you may not be getting any deductions there. In retirement, much of your income may be taxable, and you may have no deductions available to you.

Wouldn't it be better to build "exit strategies" to give yourself tax deductions or leverage in retirement? Exit strategies can give you the ability to take some money out of your retirement plan without paying the full amount of taxes that would ordinarily be due. If you could employ some complementary strategies to offer you current and/or future tax deductions, they would prove very valuable in retirement.

How many tax-efficient levers will you be able to pull to help you in retirement?

If you plan correctly, you can have more security and comfort in those later years, when security is most needed, wanted and possibly critical for you to enjoy the rest of your life. Sometimes, it's not even a different product that may offer you an amazing method of getting more income or more use of your money. Instead, it comes down to how the products can work together to produce a greater result. It's knowing how to use the different tools you may own or should own to create a better outcome.

This is critical. I find it advantageous to educate clients about some of these possibilities while they are in their 40s or 5Os, instead of waiting until they're in their 60s or 70s. This way you can set the stage for some of these possibilities early on. There are things you need to do now to make some of these tax-efficient levers available later. Don't wait until you're in your 60s or 70s to learn what you wish you knew in your 40s or 5Os. (For more on this, please see Chapter 11, "Does Charity Really Begin at Home?")

Chapter 9

Succession vs. Forced Liquidation

hat's your business succession plan? When you're
ready to let your business go, or if you're no longer
alive or healthy enough to run the business, what
happens next? Is the business sold to your partners? Do you leave
it to your children? Sell it to a competitor?

Or is there no current plan? If so, your heirs have only one
option—if something happens to you, then they must sell the
business for whatever they can get. If you stay alive, then perhaps
as some point you will try to sell the business and see what you
get. But that's just hope, and it isn't grounded in reality.

So many successful entrepreneurs I have worked with over
the years had no real plan, and therefore no real options. Life is

unpredictable. It's so full of curve balls that you surely cannot plan for every possible event. However, there are many planning options that allow for flexibility and creativity later on, when you might need or want it.

If you're in the minority and you've already put in place different agreements and funding for those agreements, are they reasonably up-to-date? I ask because so often, I see outdated partnership agreements and outdated funding arrangements for those agreements. Years go by so quickly, and company valuations change all the time. Is your business worth more today than it was five or ten years ago? No doubt. But without updated valuations and funding for these types of agreements, somebody will be very unhappy. Don't let this be your family!

If your thoughts are to leave the business to your children, what contingencies are in place to allow that to happen effectively? The sorry statistic is that *70 percent of all second generation businesses fail.*

Why is that?

New owners make mistakes. Clients and customers, used to the founder's ways of doing things, may leave. These things can be detrimental to the running of a business.

Think about it: I'm sure you've made some mistakes along the way. We all have. With some planning and preparation, though, there are ways to ensure that a smooth transition from your leadership to that of the next generation takes place, and that the business can continue and even thrive.

Most entrepreneurs I know have worked very hard to build their business. It just doesn't make sense to leave things to chance. Invest a little time, effort, and money to put contingencies in place to ensure your desires and intentions for the business to actually come to fruition.

Do you have children who work in the business, as well as children who are not involved in the business?

What is your plan for an equitable inheritance, should something happen to you?

"Equitable" and "equal" are not necessarily the same thing. I recently helped a client in this very situation—trying to decide what "fair" meant for the family.

The client's overall estate is valued at approximately $10 million. The business is valued at approximately $5 million—50 percent of the entire estate. The son has worked in the business for over 17 years and has labored to help grow the business with many late nights and long weeks. While he has been in the business working hard, the value of the business has increased nicely.

So the parents were thinking about giving the business to their son. But what about their daughter who has never worked in the business? She is married with twins, and all the while her husband has a completely different avocation with a reasonable salary.

What's equitable?

What's fair?

If they decide to give the business to the son and the other half of their estate to their daughter—is that fair?

I don't think so. The son has dedicated all his working years to the business. He's really earned some of the company stock through his blood, sweat, and tears.

By talking through these issues, we helped the family map out solutions.

One possible solution is for the son to buy half of the business over time through some of the cash flow the business generates, with the other half to be deemed an inheritance.

The son and daughter can equally inherit 50 percent of the $5 million in non-business assets, and $2.5 million of the business interest (50 percent of the approximate value).

They each would inherit a value of $3,750,000 and the son would buy the other half of the business interest through the cash flow provided by the business, which he works hard to maintain and grow. If something should happen to the parents before the son has completely bought half of the business shares, there is life insurance in place to provide the funds needed to complete the buy-out.

All parties are now protected, and now neither child feels they got cheated. It's reasonably equitable to all involved parties.

It gives parents peace of mind to know that after they're gone, their kids will stay close. They would hate for their children to be arguing or fighting over money, as that ruins many relationships. Talking through these issues ahead of time eliminates the stress that so often overwhelms family relationships.

We recommend having a family meeting at some point to discuss the business continuity and estate plan with all involved parties. This is a great way to field all objectives, questions, and concerns so all family members are on the same page. Family cohesiveness is so important—something not to be left to chance.

Every situation is different, but all of these factors really need to be considered before drawing up legal documents that most people don't even understand.

I always recommend flow-charting what the business continuity and estate plan is going to look like. Once we do the flow chart, our clients can understand how their plan will work. Again, the goal here is to have your wishes carried out and for everyone involved to understand the plan.

Chapter 10
Building the Future of Your Estate

state planning doesn't mean you are planning to die, or you are planning to give away or lock up all of your assets. Estate planning is basically devising a plan for who you would like to inherit what and when if something happens to you, your spouse, or both— and then putting that plan down on paper. You're deciding how the money is going to be distributed—in what manner, over what time period, with what checks and balances. You also want to do that with the least taxes, costs and family hassles while making the plan as equitable as possible.

The goal in most cases is to keep your money where it belongs: with those you love.

The idea is to develop a plan around your wishes. Having your desires and wishes carried out correctly may be simple, or it can be more complicated. A critical part of this is how your assets are owned. You may have drafted a spectacular will, but if your assets are not titled correctly, the will won't work. That may sound crazy, but it's true. As we've discussed, the coordination of wills and the titling of assets is absolutely critical for your will to work in the way you want.

Another challenge is that the government is always changing the laws on estate taxes. Estate tax laws have been changed many times in our nation's history. It started in 1898, when the government was taxing estates greater than or equal to $10,000. In 1916, it moved to only estates valued more than $50,000. The estate tax was repealed in 1926, and then reinstated in 1932. The government went back and forth on the tax rates and on what estate values should be taxable. A 15 percent excise tax on having too much money in qualified pension plans was added, which lasted until 1997. Then, you guessed it—that tax was repealed. In 2010, a two-year provision was instituted to raise the allowable amount of money one could transfer without taxes to $5 million. In 2012, it was raised to $5.12 million, to $5.25 million in 2013, and to $5.34 million in 2014. The number is indexed for inflation.

Do you really think it won't change again?

It's also important to remember that the estate tax rates and amount of assets that avoid taxes in your state are different than those of the federal government, and generally much lower. percent. Sometimes the entrepreneurs we work with are unaware of these potential additional estate taxes.[5]

There are several methods for discounting the taxable estate values of the many assets you may own or acquire. Attorneys can create separate legal entities to accomplish this. You can gift some shares while you still control the assets or majority interest and the majority of the revenue. An estate planning attorney may recommend a family limited partnership, or a limited liability company (LLC). There are many of different ways to do this, and it can get complicated to have it done correctly. You definitely need to map everything out and then meet with a good estate planning attorney to get it right. There are some phenomenal trust designs that can protect the financial world you've worked hard to build from divorce and creditors. I call that "Bloodline Protection."

It is definitely not a case of one size fits all. You really need to understand the flow of assets and income in all of these potential scenarios. There are some great methods to ensure that you can pass on a legacy of significance, but there are also some types of restrictions and complications of which you need to be aware.

Below are some common mistakes people make when thinking about estate planning:

1. You don't think you have enough money to do estate planning. But as you may have seen from the chapter on

---

5   The charitable income tax deduction is calculated based on life
     expectancy, assumed interest earned on money in the trust, and the
     chosen annual withdrawal rate.

protection, you always need to protect who is in your life and what assets you have built or acquired.

2. Outdated wills and trusts may name people to be guardians, trustees, or executors who you may not even talk to anymore or who you may not like or trust anymore. This happens all the time, but it could become a huge problem if not fixed before something unforeseen happens.

3. Don't lock up or lose access to your money or lose the ability to use your money to make more money. You really want to able to control your money and assets so you can use them to the fullest extent of their capabilities.

4. Don't jump on the 'second-to-die' life insurance bandwagon so quickly (something will talk about in more detail shortly). Life insurance is an integral part of most estate plans, but there are many different strategies and they are vastly different with vastly different outcomes.

It is very hard to know when you are in your 40s, 50s, or even 60s what assets you will want or need when you are in your 70s, 80s, or 90s. It would be guesswork at best, and I feel employing guesswork is no way to plan. This is why it's important to have flexibility—including being able to continue estate planning after the first spouse passes away.

Often, when one spouse passes away, the surviving spouse is in their 70s or 80s. At that point in your life, you will have a much better idea of what your finances look like than when you were doing your initial estate planning in your 40s or 50s. In your 70s or 80s, you may know what assets you need and what assets you do not. It makes much more sense to be able to gift to your children or grandchildren later in life when you have a much better idea as to how much money you still need or want in retirement, and what assets you don't need anymore.

The other aspect of being able to plan in this way is that it allows you the possibility of making large gifts to your children while one spouse is alive. There are many benefits to this approach. First, when you remove an asset from your estate, the future growth of that asset is no longer in your estate. Your children don't have to wait until both you and your spouse are gone to enjoy some of the fruits of your labor, and you can see them enjoy using some of those resources for themselves. It also can be a great way for your children to pay significantly less money in estate taxes.

To me, this is a much better option. "Second-to-die" life insurance *does not* give you that option. You lose all flexibility along with a potential magnitude of savings and estate leveraging.

Let's look at a hypothetical example: Steve and Mary Jones. Let's say Steve passes away in his 70s and Mary lives 14 years longer than her husband (which is the statistical average). For simplicity's sake, I will use a 50 percent federal estate rate. At the time you read this, the actual rate may be higher or lower depending on how many times the government has changed the rates after this book's publication.

So, by the time that Mary passes away in her mid-80s, we will assume the Joneses had a $20 million taxable estate, after all credits and deductions at a 50 percent estate tax rate. This means their kids would pay $10 million in taxes and then inherit $10 million. That is a high cost for an inheritance!

Now, some financial planners, estate planners, and insurance agents advise buying $10 million of 'second-to-die' life insurance and letting the insurance pay the tax. That could definitely help, and would cover that tax if that is what the tax ended up being 20, 30, or 40 years after they bought the policy.

But let's look at a different option. This is where it is important to know the difference between gift taxes and estate taxes. They are not the same thing. They carry the same tax rate, but are vastly different in terms of transferring wealth.

Let's say that after Steve passed away, Mary realized that she could afford to gift a building she owned to her children. She can do this because she does not need the rental income anymore. Maybe she can gift their family's vacation home for a total asset value of $10 million while she's still alive. The gift tax in this example would be $5 million. Gift tax is 50 percent tax on the amount gifted; the same tax rate as estate taxes, but the results are very different.

In the case of gifting, it costs $15 million to pass $10 million of assets to their children, rather than the $20 million in the previous example with estate taxes. That's $5 million less by gifting assets instead of waiting to pay estate taxes. Big difference, right? Here's how it works:

Passing wealth to heirs – Inclusive versus Exclusive

Estate Tax = Inclusive	Gift Tax = Exclusive
Heirs inherit $20,000,000	Grantor gifts $10,000,000 to Heirs
Heirs pay 50% Estate Tax* ($10,000,000)	Grantor pays 50% Gift Tax ($5,000,000)
$10,000,000 net to Heirs	$10,000,000 net to Heirs
Total cost for heirs to receive $10,000,000…	Total cost for heirs to receive $10,000,000…
$20,000,000	**$15,000,000**

HOCHHEISER DEUTSCH & company inc.   *Estate tax rates are subject to change -currently 40% Federal (has been as high as 55%) + your state tax rates could be anywhere from 6-8% currently

Now, let's bring insurance into the discussion. If Steve and Mary had bought a 'second-to-die' life insurance policy, nothing happens after Steve dies—except that Mary still has to continue paying premiums and no insurance proceeds come in. After something like this happens, the widow or widower always wants to know why they have to keep paying the premiums and why there are not any life insurance proceeds now.

If they had 'first-to-die' insurance, and Steve passed away, Mary could use the $10 million of insurance to pay the gift tax that was due, which only amounts to $5 million. Then, there is still $5 million left that Mary could either use or leave in an account or in a trust if that was where the life insurance was owned. Now, the future growth of that remaining $5 million could be quite large, and if it were in a trust, it would still be outside of the estate. Alternatively, Mary could gift $20 million of assets if she had it and didn't need it, and just use all of the insurance to pay the gift tax. It might be nice for Mary to see her children and grandchildren benefiting from the rental income the building throws off since she doesn't need it any more. Maybe she would take some of the insurance proceeds and pay for all of her grandchildren's education, or help them with a down payment for a house.

Mary has so many good options, and she is under no pressure to do anything. There may even be some great new strategies available that weren't available when Mary and Steve were drafting their wills and trusts 20, 30, or 40 years prior. Who knows?

What we do know is that options are good, saving millions of your hard-earned dollars is great—and giving more to your family and less to the IRS is priceless.

It's all about having flexibility, and you get none of that flexibility with 'second-to-die' life insurance. You get a cheaper bill, and that's about all there is to be happy about.

The goal is to have the best lifestyle possible in retirement and to enjoy the wealth you have built. As such, you should put yourself in a position to transfer that wealth to who you want, when you want, with the smallest amount of taxes and fees. I don't see how you can do that without options and flexibility later on in life. There is no way to predict how you can do that 20, 30, or 40 years in advance. Most people miss this need for flexibility, and may pass on significantly less wealth because of it. Many future generations will possess less wealth and less enjoyment of that wealth because of an initial lack of flexibility.

Many entrepreneurs we have worked with desire to pass along a legacy of significance and protect their wealth not only for themselves, but for future generations as well. Keeping the wealth that you have worked so hard to build in the bloodline is what I call "Bloodline Protection." With the right methods of planning and the right advisory team, you can execute a great estate plan with confidence and clarity knowing you have done the best you could for your family.

Chapter 11

Does Charity Really Begin at Home?

Let's discuss some charitable planning strategies that can be amazing for you to employ in retirement. Some of them will give you tax deductions that may be quite large, and others will reduce the value of your taxable estate or allow you to transfer more wealth with less tax—and, of course, help some of the charities that may be close to your heart.

Many successful entrepreneurs are focused on giving back when they can, and trying to help society as a whole, and therefore have multiple charitable interests. So it seems natural to me that if they were aware of some mutually beneficial charitable strategies that could help a charity while providing greater cash flow and paying less taxes, they would be all over it. There may be charitable strategies that would be a good fit—and when done correctly, usually the only the IRS loses out.

Here's one charitable tool that you can use to knock down your taxes: the charitable remainder trust (CRT). Let's say you have a building that's worth two million dollars. You bought it years ago for half a million. Every year, you depreciate the building. You want to sell it when you retire because you don't want to deal with collecting rent, but there's no basis left because of the depreciation. So if you sell it for two million, you'll probably pay about six hundred thousand dollars in combined federal and state capital gains taxes. Included is also the 3.8 percent Medicare tax, leaving you with $1.4 million. Or, you could take that building and put it in a charitable trust. If you sell it when it's in the trust, you'll pay no capital gains tax. Now you have two million to invest and you'll get income for life. The difference is that when the husband and wife die, the money in that trust doesn't go to the kids—it goes to charity.

The amount that goes to charity is called the "remainder interest," and because of this "remainder interest," you qualify for a tax deduction, which in this example might be around $1.5 million. This could save you another $600,000 in taxes. So now you get income for life on the full $2 million, *plus* that additional tax deduction for $1.5 million. That adds up to approximately $1 million of tax savings on a $2 million asset.

The tax deductions that the charitable remainder trust generates could be used to offset some of the tax you would pay on withdrawing your pension plan or 401(k) assets. In that case, you can get a deduction when the 401(k) pension money goes in, and if designed properly, it's possible to avoid some of the nasty taxes on the way out. Now that's an exit strategy! Please consult with your tax advisor regarding your own personal situation.

As in other matters, you'll need an expert trust and estate attorney for your estate planning documents. You need the same person to create the best charitable strategies for your specific situation.

The charity wins. The parents win. The kids don't get that asset, but you can ensure they receive life insurance or a different asset. If they get insurance for that $2 million, they're just as happy as getting the actual building. In fact, it might be even better. Only the IRS loses out, and I'm sure you're just fine with that.

Chapter 12

How Would You Describe YOUR Advisory Team?

I n order to maximize your financial potential, you cannot afford to waste any financial resources along the way. You need to be taking a macro-manager approach to overseeing the big picture and be sure to have all of your advisors and financial strategies on the same page and working together on your behalf.

You need someone to take the role of the quarterback. This person will need to have a handle on all of the moving pieces and provide the coordination I have been discussing. You will need a great CPA, a great attorney and a great financial strategist. Then, once you get a second opinion on all of the financial products and strategies you have been employing along the way, you will get an idea of who else you may want on your team. To achieve financial freedom and to maximize your wealth potential, you need to have an amazing advisory team. As I asked earlier, when's the last time all of your advisors were in the room with you talking about you and your family? In many cases, the answer is never. In some cases, there is some coordination, but is "some" really good enough? Many advisors don't have the vision or the specialty of taking a holistic approach to guide entrepreneurs in building and distributing wealth that can be enjoyed through all financial stages of their lives. That is one of the major aspects we focus on.

THE MACRO-MANAGER APPROACH

The entire team should have one focus: to help you and your family the most with the least amount of time spent on your end. The team members should be working behind the scenes with your best interests in mind, and bringing you in the fold to discuss strategies, recommendations, and the best outcomes.

When I work with entrepreneurs, I take them through our Business and Professional Practice Advantage. First, we go over the basics. What kind of benefits package do they have? What kind of retirement plans are in place? How much money are they taking out of the business to achieve their personal wealth goals? Are they taking bonuses? How are they generating personal wealth from their business? It's quite possible that they can take more money out by putting a few hundred-thousand dollars into a defined benefit plan or into another savings and investment plan. The second aspect is business continuity planning. Let's say the business has partners. Is there a buy/sell agreement in place so that if something happens to one of the partners, we know what will happen with the shares of the business? Is there insurance funding that purchase? Is it the right amount of insurance, is it the right type, and is it coordinated properly? So often I've seen businesses with a buy/sell agreement stating that the stock goes to the corporation and that the other shareholder has a right to buy it back. That's great, but the problem is that the agreement might have been made when the business was worth two million dollars. Now it's worth twenty million, and the agreement hasn't been updated. I see this all the time. So the question we ask is, how do we help you build personal wealth, protect the business, and do business continuity planning so that you and your partners are secure?

The goal is to make sure that everyone is on the same page, taking care of you, and also doing what is necessary behind the scenes in a coordinated fashion. This should alleviate the time that you would need to spend on the nitty-gritty, when it's probably not your first choice of activity.

Chapter 13

The Ideal Financial Plan And The Worry-Free Retirement

hile we don't live in an ideal world, you should know the elements that are present in an ideal financial plan:

- **You have an automated systematic flow of money into your plan.** Your wealth-building engine needs fuel or it won't go very far. You need to be feeding your financial plan.

- **You have a guaranteed rate of return.** It's hard to spend 'maybes' in retirement. Having guarantees with some of your funds definitely eases stress in periods of market volatility.

- **You have accessibility to the money, should you need or want some of it or all of it.** Unforeseen events happen all the time. You don't want to be locked out of your money. It always seems to be that when you need some funds, they may not be available. Call it Murphy's Law. Make sure you don't fall victim to it.

- **There are minimum taxes on the money as it accumulates and grows.** This is very important, as we have discussed. The pain of paying so much in taxes is not only frustrating, but the compound effect of taxes also takes boatloads of money away from you and your family.

- **There are minimum taxes on the money when you take it out.** Having to pay taxes on money you are withdrawing in retirement is downright depressing, as you will likely not earn more money to replace the money that is lost.

- **You are able to minimize losses due to market volatility.** Market volatility when withdrawing funds can cripple a financial plan. If you have analyzed or seen the effects of this, you know how dramatically it can change your retirement lifestyle:

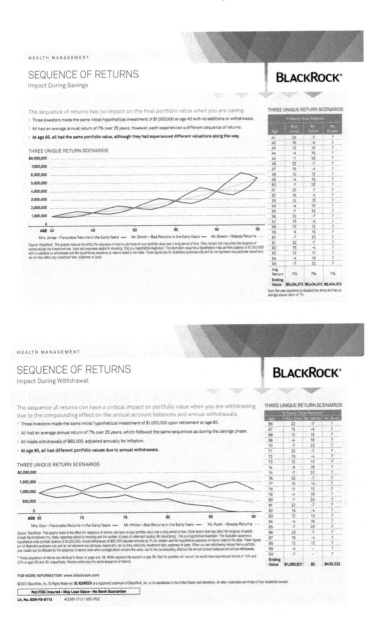

- **Your plan is self-completing in the event you become disabled and can't work.** This provides great financial balance. Having a plan in place that does this is a huge win.
- **You have flexibility to adjust and change your plan when warranted or needed.** The only constant in life is change. So much is open to change in your practice, in your finances, and in tax laws. Be prepared to deal with it by having flexibility.
- **Your money is protected from creditors[6] and as many eroding factors as possible.** Between inflation, creditors, and tax law changes, it is critical to shelter your wealth today.

The real goal is to have your financial plan successful under every possible circumstance, including if taxes go up, if interest rates go down, or if the stock market crashes.

This is what you and your advisory team should be working towards. And that work starts now, not later. All roads should lead to this. Having a worry-free retirement is your reward for working hard and planning smart. At this point, it is all about having safe, reliable, consistent income sources in retirement. That is what everyone wants and that is what retirement should be like.

---

6   Not all states have creditor protection for life insurance policies. You should contact your state's insurance department or consult your legal advisor regarding your individual situation.

The Worry-Free Retirement

Risks in Retirement

- Longevity Risk
- Market Risk/Principal Risk
- Interest Rate Risk
- Inflation
- Higher Income taxes and Public Policy Risks
- Sequence of Returns Risk
- Needing more money to live on than you thought
- Children/Parents need unexpected financial assistance
- Hubris-excessive Pride

- Disabled before having a chance to build enough wealth
- Forced Retirement
- Re-employment Risk
- Prolonged illness
- Health exp. & health insurance exp.
- Long term care expenses
- Running out of money as you get older
- Timing Risk
- Unplanned events
- Lack of Stewardship

Ideal Goals in Retirement

- Stability
- Predictability
- Tax free income
- Contingency Plans
- Capability to create leverage

- Ease of use
- Creditor protection
- Still get tax benefits & tax reducing strategies
- No stress or Financial Worries
- Financial flexibility

It's not necessarily about how much money you have but what types of assets you have and how you can most effectively use them.

Helping To Provide Financial Freedom For Successful Professionals And Entrepreneurs HOCHHEISER, DEUTSCH & Company Inc

I believe you always should have this in focus and in your thoughts when making any kind of financial decisions early on. You and your advisory team can make it happen!

Chapter 14

The Financial Freedom Scorecard™

How are you measuring your progress? And how can you be sure you are making enough financial progress every year?

The reality is that you have to keep score in order to monitor and improve upon the progress you're making.

"That which gets measured improves; that which gets measured and reported improves exponentially." –Karl Pearson

Many of our clients were doing well when they came to us, but now they are doing even better, all because they started to keep score.

Are you doing as well as you should be—or could be?

There is so much hype today surrounding credit scores, which is all about borrowing money and paying interest to someone else and making *them* wealthy. Your Financial Freedom Score™ is about *you and your family* being financially secure and wealthy. And that should be the priority.

Are you ready to establish your Financial Freedom? Go to our website, www.HDCI.biz, and click on the Financial Freedom Scorecard™ tab. Or, if you want to take the shortcut, type in www.thefinancialfreedomscorecard.com and go directly to the page. Be sure to check out the video, "Why the Scorecard," to learn more about the process. Then, get your score! Take the Scorecard now to find out how you're really doing.

Remember…winners keep score! Start keeping a tally, and tracking your success.

Chapter 15

The Choice Is ...
There Is No Choice

We have been talking about many uncoordinated, unsubstantiated financial products purchased over time, many without accurate measurements of success. How could you possibly compare a systematic, holistic process to simply purchasing a product and hoping it works out?

You cannot. Imagine going out and buying the newest golf club—a new driver, let's say. It might help your game a just because of the improved technology. But in reality, is it is not going to drop your handicap by 5, 10, or 15 strokes. The driver is what is known as the product. Now, let's say instead of buying that new driver, you invested in some lessons and a very good teacher, worked on your swing, and improved your game. That process would have universal applications and could make a big difference in your golf game.

Of course, it is much easier to go out and just buy a new club rather than spend time on lessons and practicing, but the results are also very different. The same is true for your finances—only more so. After all, buying the wrong financial products could result in much worse ramifications then hitting a slice, a hook, or hitting a ball in the water. The penalties could be much more severe with the wrong financial products or strategies.

You need a process to coordinate, organize, and integrate all strategies, products, and advisors. This coordination allows you to have the flexibility to adjust and change the plan when it's warranted.

This is what we offer in our comprehensive holistic approach, called The Financial Freedom Experience®. It is comprised of three proven, powerful and trademarked processes all aimed at providing education on how financial products and strategies really work, implementing strategies to help you grow and utilize your wealth in the most tax efficient manner, and, most of all, protecting your wealth.

How Secure is Your Life's Work?

Are you taking advantage of every opportunity in your business to create greater personal wealth? Our process, The Business and Professional Practice Advantage™, looks to do just that. You also should be integrating your personal strategies with those in your business to create a cohesive plan. In addition, you want to protect the interests of all key members of your business to be sure that all families are protected now and in the future.

Three steps to greater wealth and security is the focus of our process called The L.I.F.E. Approach™. That stands for Lifelong Improvements for Financial Empowerment. Above all else, this unique and powerful approach helps to ensure that you and your family will be protected now and forever.

We want to protect your family forever, in the event you can't.

We will analyze, test, and guide you on all your present and future financial strategies, giving you the clarity to help you attain your financial dreams. At the end of the process, you will feel empowered knowing you have made the right financial decisions for you and your family.

Lastly, we offer The Retirement and Estate Navigator™. Regardless of your age, it's important to take an honest and realistic look at the type of lifestyle your financial resources will provide in retirement. **The time to do that is now!**

We will provide you with a vital step-by-step process to identify and test different strategies to maximize your income in retirement. Additionally, you want to be sure to have a tax-efficient legacy plan that accomplishes all of your wishes and provides options for down the road.

Confidence and security comes from knowing you've finally taken the right steps.

But you cannot accomplish everything I have mentioned here and be guided through all of the complexities of today's and tomorrow's financial world without a thorough and holistic process.

Begin your journey to financial freedom now!

It only takes about 90 minutes to get you on the road to financial freedom. We have an initial meeting that we call The Financial Freedom Discovery Session™. It's a meeting that gets you on the road to financial freedom. You can go to our web site at www. HDCI.biz and email a request for a Financial Freedom Discovery Session™. We will schedule the session with you and get you started. Or you can email us at info@hdci.biz.

It's really a lot easier than you may think. We will educate you and guide you all along the way.

Investing 90 minutes could be the difference between having security, financial balance, and enjoyment by achieving financial freedom, or being frustrated by your lack of options and losing out by not harnessing the full power of your resources.

We make a huge difference in entrepreneurs' lives and the lives of their families. It's something that makes us feel great about what we do. We help you be protected and we look out for you by making sure that you are doing the right things at the right times for yourself and your family.

Our worthy ideal is to inspire and guide families to protect themselves from life's uncertainties, to safeguard and grow their wealth so they have the freedom to enjoy life with financial clarity and confidence.

We've done a lot to help entrepreneurs enjoy their retirement, buy their vacation homes, protect their loved ones, send their kids to college, and do it all in an efficient format that creates the best lifestyle now and in the future for them and their families to enjoy. This is what we stand for and why we do what we do. I wish you and your family all the success in life and I hope I have the privilege of meeting you in person to add to it.

Now that you know the possibilities for your financial freedom, you're probably wondering what steps you can take in order to achieve that vision. And that's exactly what I will leave you with—actions you can take right away to transform your financial outlook.

Five Things You Must Do Now to Achieve Financial Freedom

1. It is imperative that you are absolutely sure you are fully protected from life's uncertainties by reviewing your protection components annually.

2. You must review and monitor your overall long-term savings rates annually to be sure you are on pace for saving 15-20 percent of your gross income.

3. On an annual basis, you must assess how you're building wealth in the 3 Pools of Money, and what the 3 Pools will look like later. Do you have a good balance?

4. You must be sure your estate and business continuity plans are up to date, coordinated properly, and equitably structured.

5. Every year you must evaluate and continually be improving your Financial Freedom Score™.

Acknowledgements

I want to thank my family for their support and genuine interest in this book. I appreciate all of the relentless conversations we had about the book and their patience as it took much longer than I had hoped or expected.

I want to thank my team at Hochheiser, Deutsch & Company Inc. for all of their help with this book and all that they do for me and our clients every day. You are all amazing at what you do. Thank you for providing me with the time to write this book. And a special thank you to Katherine. You are just the best!

I also want to thank Dan Sullivan from The Strategic Coach. Without Dan and his wisdom and encouragement, this book would never have been written, or written in this century.

I also want to acknowledge Bob Castiglione who founded Leap Systems Inc. I had thought after I completed my Certified Financial Planning designation (CFP) in 1996 that I had great knowledge to properly assist clients in building and protecting wealth. But then I met Bob Castiglione. Bob has taught me so much about measuring the true economics of many financial decisions. He truly opened my eyes and dramatically added to my knowledge and capability in assisting our clients.

I also want to thank Bob Ball, who was formally with Leap Systems and now consults on the continual development of The Living Balance Sheet®.[7] He is largely responsible for its continued success. Bob Ball has continued to add to my professional development over the years and I am very fortunate to have his support and his friendship.

I also owe a debt of gratitude to Rick Wollman of Empowered Mastery Consultants for all of his marketing input and help throughout the last few years. Rick, you have helped us transform our communication so everyone knows who we really are, what we really do, and who we do it for. Thank you!

The quotes on the back cover represent the personal views of a select group of Jay Hochheiser's clients and may not represent the experience of other clients. The opinions are not indicative of future performance or results.

---

7   The Living Balance Sheet® (LBS) and the LBS logo are registered service marks of The Guardian Life Insurance Company of America (Guardian), New York, NY. © Copyright 2005-2016. The Guardian Life Insurance Company of America.